# Good Housekeeping

# SIMPLE VEGAN!

## DELICIOUS MEAT-FREE, DAIRY-FREE RECIPES EVERY FAMILY WILL LOVE

### HEARST BOOKS
A division of Sterling Publishing Co., Inc.

New York / London
www.sterlingpublishing.com

## GOOD HOUSEKEEPING

Rosemary Ellis
**EDITOR IN CHIEF**

Sara Lyle
**LIFESTYLE EDITOR**

Susan Westmoreland
**FOOD DIRECTOR**

Samantha B. Cassetty, M.S., R.D.
**NUTRITION DIRECTOR**

Sharon Franke
**FOOD APPLIANCES DIRECTOR**

**BOOK DESIGN** by Memo Productions
**EDITED** by Sarah Scheffel
Photography Credits on page 158

Library of Congress
Cataloging-in-Publication Data
Good housekeeping simple vegan! : delicious
meat-free, dairy-free recipes every family
will love.
       p. cm.
  Includes index.
1. Vegan cooking. I. Good housekeeping
(New York, N.Y.) II. Title: Simple vegan!
  TX837.G648 2010
  61.5'636--dc22     2010028169

10  9  8  7  6  5  4  3  2  1

The Good Housekeeping Cookbook Seal guar-
antees that the recipes in this cookbook meet
the strict standards of the Good Housekeeping
Research Institute. The Institute has been a source
of reliable information and a consumer advocate
since 1900, and established its seal of approval
in 1909. Every recipe has been triple-tested for
ease, reliability, and great taste.

Published by Hearst Books
A division of Sterling Publishing Co., Inc.
387 Park Avenue South, New York, NY 10016

Good Housekeeping is a registered trademark of
Hearst Communications, Inc.

www.goodhousekeeping.com

For information about custom editions,
special sales, premium and corporate
purchases, please contact Sterling Special Sales
Department at 800-805-5489
or specialsales@sterlingpublishing.com.

Distributed in Canada by Sterling Publishing
c/o Canadian Manda Group, 165 Dufferin Street
Toronto, Ontario, Canada M6K 3H6

Distributed in Australia by Capricorn Link
(Australia) Pty. Ltd.
P.O. Box 704, Windsor, NSW 2756 Australia

Manufactured in China

Sterling ISBN 978-1-58816-868-9

# CONTENTS

# FOREWORD

"I'm a vegan" were words that struck fear in the heart of this young Cordon Bleu graduate back in the late 1970s. Fresh from a world of julienning, mother sauces and soufflés, I had moved into a household with a group of friends and agreed to cook once a week. What I didn't know is that I'd be cooking vegan. After a few of my friends' dinners of wallpaper-paste-like millet and barley with steamed vegetables, I decided there had to be vegan life beyond this tamari-soaked fare. And there was.

Growing up in an Italian-American family, I ate lots of truly delicious vegetable-based meals, albeit many with dairy. So, when it came time to cook without meat, seafood, or dairy, I took inspiration from my roots and prepared a pot of vegetable-rich minestrone that everyone enjoyed—me included.

These days, though I'm an omnivore, I cook a lot of meatless meals. Like you, I find that I'm not hungry for meat every night, and less meat means more room for wholesome grains and veggies. I've also learned about the rising rates of heart disease, diabetes, and concern about lactose intolerance among adults and children—so my understanding of the benefits of a vegan diet has clicked into place.

The truth is, you can prepare the dishes your family regularly enjoys—pastas and stir-fries, soups and stews, burritos, burgers, and even baked goods—vegan style. You just have to become familiar with the appropriate substitutions (see page 14 and additional tips throughout this book) and keep basic nutritional guidelines in mind (see page 11).

This collection of 100 simple and satisfying vegan recipes—all triple-tested in the Good Housekeeping Test Kitchens—is your road map to delicious vegan meals and snacks. Whether you and your family plan to eliminate all animal products from your diet, or simply eat vegan a couple nights a week, we provide recipes so good, no one will miss the meat or cheese.

The book opens with Energizing Breakfasts—from smoothies to granola and, yes, even muffins, pancakes, and waffles for Sunday brunch. Our super salads are paired with suggestions for adding extra grains and protein, and our sandwiches—from falafel to Tempeh Reubens with a homemade Thousand Island Dressing—will make lunch time as yummy as it is healthy. Our suppers span the globe with an assortment of nourishing noodle dishes, tofu stir-fries, bean and veggie-based soups, and burritos you'll be happy to present to family or friends. Plus, chapters on grilling and comfort food, vegan style, make it plain that you can create toothsome grills and creamy casseroles sans meat. Because locating a vegan snack when you need it can prove to be a challenge, we close with Savory & Sweet Treats, easy to make nibbles and snacks to have on hand when you need a little energy boost.

So whether you are embracing a true vegan lifestyle, cooking for someone who is a vegan, or simply looking for more vegetable and grain-based recipes, *Simple Vegan!* provides delicious, easy-to-make recipes that will be a welcome addition to your repertoire.

**SUSAN WESTMORELAND**
Food Director, *Good Housekeeping*

*Southwestern Black Bean Burgers (page 88)*

# WELCOME TO *SIMPLE VEGAN!*

We know you may have brought this book home for any number of reasons:

- You're a vegan and you want a collection of delicious, family-friendly recipes.
- You or a family member is switching to a vegan diet, and you need basic dietary guidelines and healthy recipes to get you started.
- Although you don't intend to eliminate all animal products from your plate, a couple nights a week, you want to serve simple vegan fare based on wholesome grains, legumes, and veggies.

Whatever your particular motivation, *Simple Vegan!* is here to help. With 100 triple-tested recipes developed in the Good Housekeeping Test Kitchens, plus advice on shopping for and preparing satisfying vegan meals, this is a book you can rely on to feed you and your family with ease and confidence.

## Good for You...

A vegan diet eliminates all animal products (meat, poultry, and fish) and products derived from animals (butter, milk, yogurt, and cheese). The bonus? This way of eating naturally encourages you and your family to fill up on good-for-you foods grown from the earth. Study after study has shown that a diet rich in whole grains, legumes, vegetables, and fruit results in numerous health benefits:

- It reduces the risk of heart disease and can have a positive effect on those who already have heart disease. Saturated fat and cholesterol are two dietary culprits that raise the risk for heart disease. Both are derived almost exclusively from animal products.
- It reduces the risk of some cancers. That's one reason the American Cancer Society recommends eating five or more servings of vegetables and fruits each day. This is easier than you might think: One serving equals 1 cup leafy vegetables or ½ cup cooked or raw vegetables, or ½ cup fruit or one medium piece of fruit.
- It can assist in weight loss and long-term weight management. That's because switching to a plant-based diet may dramatically

reduce fat and calorie intake. Although there are obese vegans (and slim meat-eaters), the American Dietetic Association reports that meat-eaters have three times the obesity rate of vegetarians and nine times the obesity rate of vegans.

Including more whole grains, legumes, vegetables, and fruits also means increasing your intake of fiber, vitamins and minerals, antioxidants, and phytochemicals. That's good news for your diet—and your health!

# HELP FOR THE LACTOSE-INTOLERANT

Lactose intolerance is an inability or insufficient ability to metabolize lactose, a sugar found in milk and milk products. It is caused by a deficiency of the enzyme lactase, which is produced by the cells lining the small intestine. Symptoms range from mild to severe digestive discomfort.

If you or a family member suffers from lactose intolerance, reduction of milk and milk products is often part of the prescribed treatment, so the dairy-free recipes in this cookbook may be a welcome addition to your family's menu. However, according to the National Institute of Health, even in persons with lactose intolerance, small amounts of milk, yogurt, hard cheeses, and reduced lactose foods may be effective management approaches. Most individuals can probably ingest 1 cup of milk daily without symptoms. Consult your doctor for the appropriate treatment for you or your lactose-intolerant family member.

## Good for Your Wallet...

Adding more produce and grains to your diet and reducing the animal products is not only good for your health, it's undeniably good for your pocketbook, too. This is especially true if you primarily prepare your meals with whole foods—grains, beans, and legumes bought in bulk and fresh vegetables and fruits rather than relying on processed canned, frozen, or otherwise packaged ingredients. But even if you rely on packaged tofu and canned beans for your protein, you'll save money.

- **Tofu vs. Chicken Breasts:** If you're looking for an economical source of protein, tofu costs 40 percent less than chicken breasts. You'll find that it's a versatile choice that can be substituted in a wide variety of your favorite stir-fries, pastas, sandwiches, and casseroles, too.
- **Beans vs. Ground Beef:** Beans can't be beat when it comes to a low-cost source of good nutrition. They are packed with protein and insoluable and soluable fiber, and unlike beef, they contain zero saturated fat and cholesterol. The good news for your wallet: You can purchase almost three cans of beans for the cost of one pound of ground beef.

But don't overlook the money-saving benefits of buying in bulk. Purchase dried beans and legumes instead of canned for one-third the cost. For convenience, cook them ahead of time using the following basic recipe, divide into 1½ cup portions (the equivalent of a 15.5-ounce can of beans), pack in airtight containers, and freeze for up to 6 months.

## HOME-COOKED BEANS

In colander, rinse **2 bags (16 ounces) dried red kidney, pinto, cannellini, or black beans** with cold water; discard any stones or shriveled beans. Soak overnight in an 8-quart saucepot with enough **water** to cover by 2 inches. Drain beans and return to saucepot. Add **1 large onion**, cut into quarters; **2 cloves garlic**, crushed with a garlic press; **2 sprigs parsley**; **2 bay leaves**; and **6 cups water**; heat to boiling on high. Reduce heat to medium-low; partially cover and simmer 45 to 60 minutes or until beans are tender, stirring occasionally. Drain beans and discard parsley and bay leaf. Makes 10 to 12 cups.

**EACH ½-CUP SERVING:** ABOUT 260 CALORIES | 17G PROTEIN
48G CARBOHYDRATE | 1G TOTAL FAT (0G SATURATED) | 12G FIBER
0MG CHOLESTEROL | 10MG SODIUM

## Good for the Planet...

Many people are reducing their consumption of animal products for reasons that extend far beyond their waistlines. They know that following a vegan diet not only delivers individual health benefits, it helps ensure a healthier planet for future generations. Consider the following facts:

- **Feeding more people:** It takes more land, water, and energy to produce meat than to grow vegetables and grains. In fact, a study by the World Hunger Program at Brown University found that if we all got 25 percent of our calories from animal products, the global food supply would feed 3.16 billion people, whereas, if we all followed a vegetarian diet, we could produce enough food to feed almost twice as many people—6.26 billion! World hunger is a complicated problem, and eating vegan here in the U.S. won't necessarily alleviate it in the short-term, but many people have decided they want to consume more grains themselves instead of feeding them to cows to produce beef.
- **For the love of animals:** You've heard it in the news: Once upon a time, farm animals were raised on small family farms, where they grazed on pastureland or ate locally grown feed, and were slaughtered by the same farmer who took care of them. But the competition to produce inexpensive meat, eggs, and dairy products has replaced these small farms with factory farms—large warehouses where animals are raised in confined quarters and treated with antibiotics to avoid the spread of diseases, then shipped off to giant slaughterhouses. Concerned about the treatment of these farm animals and the quality of the products raised on these farms, many people have decided to avoid meat and dairy produced in factory farms by buying locally produced, often organic, alternatives or by eliminating meat and dairy from their diets altogether.

So, when you pass up a beef burger in favor of a veggie burger, you are not only keeping your cholesterol levels down, in a small way, you are helping to ensure the health and well-being of your world.

# Nutritional Guidelines for Vegans

If you or someone in your family (especially growing children) is eliminating meat and dairy from their diet, according to the United States Department of Agriculture, there are several nutrients you need to pay particular attention to:

**Protein** Protein is involved in most every type of cell function in the human body, including the production of antibodies and hemoglobin. When a child tells mom that she's going to be a vegan, it's usually protein Mom is most worried about. But there is no need; there are plenty of plant-based sources for protein. Here are a few: beans and pulses (including split peas, lentils, garbanzo beans, black beans, and pinto beans), nuts and nut butters, peas, and soy products such as tofu, tempeh, and soy milk (just be sure to check the package's nutrition label; the amount of protein in soy milk varies from brand to brand).

**Calcium** The mineral calcium is used for building bones and teeth; it is also important for maintaining bone strength. Sources of calcium for those following a vegan diet include soybeans and soy-based products like tofu and calcium-enriched soy milk, and calcium-fortified orange juice. When it comes to calcium and tofu, calcium content varies from brand to brand, so read the label. Also, tofu made using calcium sulfate will contain more calcium than tofu made using nigari (magnesium chloride). Some dark leafy greens like bok choy and collard, turnip, and mustard greens also contain calcium, but it is significantly less readily absorbed by the body, and thus should not be relied on as a primary source for calcium.

**Iron** The mineral iron is essential because it enables red blood cells to carry oxygen throughout the body. There are two types of iron in food. One is found in meat and fish and is readily absorbed. The other type of iron is plant-based, which is less well absorbed. However, when plant-based iron-rich foods are consumed in tandem with foods containing vitamin C (or if a particular food contains both iron and vitamin C, like Swiss chard), the absorption rate of the iron increases significantly. Many vegetables contain both (see the list below), but you

## PLANT-BASED VEGETABLES WITH IRON AND VITAMIN C

For better absorption of iron, eat foods like the following that contain both iron and vitamin C.

- Beet greens
- Brussels sprouts
- Fortified cereals
- Garbanzo beans
- Green peas
- Kale
- Lentils
- Parsley
- Shiitake mushrooms
- Soybeans
- Spinach
- Swiss chard
- Wheat bran

can also create your own combinations, for example by simmering iron-rich tofu in a vitamin C-rich tomato sauce, or by adding vitamin C-packed bell peppers to a lentil-bean salad or a dish that contains the grain quinoa.

**Zinc** While the body does not need much zinc, what it does need is vital for good health. Zinc is necessary for many biochemical reactions and also helps the immune system function properly. Sources of zinc include many types of beans (chickpeas, white beans, and kidney beans to name a few), pumpkin and sesame seeds, wheat germ, and zinc-fortified breakfast cereals.

**Vitamin B$_{12}$** Vitamin B$_{12}$ is vital to red blood cell production, as well as the development of nerve cells. It is predominantly derived from meat and fish products. In a vegan diet, it can be found in nutritional yeast, as well as B$_{12}$-fortified products such as cereal, soymilk, and some veggie burgers (check your labels).

To reap maximum health benefits, your meals and snacks should be based on nourishing whole foods (beans, grains, veggies, and fruits) rather than processed or prepacked items. However, throughout the book, we've provided tips on selecting vegan substitutions for meat, cheese, and dairy products that you can incorporate into your family's diet in small amounts for flavor and fun. See Vegan Dairy and Egg Substitutes, below.

## Eat and Enjoy!

Whatever your reasons for wanting to cook meat-free, dairy-free recipes, we invite you to explore the tasty selection of dishes we've assembled for you in *Simple Vegan!* In addition to a wide range of main dishes—from soups and stir-fries to pasta dishes, pizzas, and even entrées prepared on the grill—we've included a chapter on savory nibbles and sweet treats to help make snacking vegan style convenient and satisfying.

## VEGAN DAIRY AND EGG SUBSTITUTES

The Internet provides such easy access to health and whole food stores, it's a great time to be a vegan. Use it to research specific food products and where they are sold. Here's a sample list of some of the dairy- and egg-alternative products currently available:

- Nondairy margarine, including soy margarine
- Soy milk, rice milk, and nut milks (including almond and cashew milk)
- Nondairy soy sour cream and cream cheese
- Nondairy rice-, soy-, and coconut milk-based yogurts
- Nondairy heavy cream
- Nondairy soy frozen yogurt
- Nondairy soy- and coconut milk-based ice creams
- Nondairy chocolate (chocolate typically contains milk solids; see A Guide to Chocolate, page 149)
- Egg-free soy mayonnaise
- Egg replacements (check vegan and vegetarian websites for recommended substitutions)

*Gazpacho with Cilantro Cream (page 98)*

# ENERGIZING BREAKFASTS

Rise and shine! This chapter contains a delicious selection of vegan breakfast and brunch options that are well worth waking up for, plus tips on vegan substitutions for eggs and milk.

If you're looking for quick and easy, search no further. For a perfect on-the-go breakfast, try our smoothies, which feature a bonanza of fruit plus your choice of nondairy milk or yogurt (see Guide to Nondairy Milk, page 25). Warming 5-Minute Multigrain Cereal, low-fat granola, and carrot cake muffins will also get you out the door in a jiffy—with a healthy dose of dietary fiber to keep you feeling satisfied until lunchtime.

On weekends, when a more leisurely pace is possible, treat family and friends to our South-of-the-Border Vegetable Hash or Tofu Scramble with Chopped Tomatoes and Chives. These brunch entrées are so yummy, no one will be looking for the cheese omelet. And, yes, you can eat your fill of pancakes and waffles, too—choose whole grain, pumpkin, or pecan. Then bring out the maple syrup and grab a fork!

*Pomegranate-Berry Smoothie (page 18)*

# ORANGE SUNRISE SMOOTHIE

Make this once and you'll want it to start all your mornings.

---

**TOTAL TIME:** 5 MINUTES

**MAKES:** 1¾ CUPS OR 1 SERVING

---

| | | | |
|---|---|---|---|
| 1 | CUP VANILLA SOY MILK | 2 | TABLESPOONS ORANGE MARMALADE |
| ¼ | CUP FROZEN ORANGE JUICE CONCENTRATE | 2 | ICE CUBES |

In blender, combine soy milk, orange juice concentrate, marmalade, and ice, and blend until mixture is smooth and frothy. Pour into a tall glass.

---

**EACH SERVING:** ABOUT 360 CALORIES | 8G PROTEIN | 73G CARBOHYDRATE | 5G TOTAL FAT (0G SATURATED) | 2G FIBER | 0MG CHOLESTEROL | 144MG SODIUM

# POMEGRANATE-BERRY SMOOTHIE

A delicious and healthful breakfast. Berries and pomegranates are loaded with heart-healthy antioxidants. (For photo, see page 16.)

---

**TOTAL TIME:** 5 MINUTES

**MAKES:** 2 CUPS OR 1 SERVING

---

| | | | |
|---|---|---|---|
| ½ | CUP POMEGRANATE JUICE, CHILLED | 1 | CUP FROZEN MIXED BERRIES |
| ½ | CUP NONDAIRY VANILLA YOGURT | | |

In blender, combine juice, yogurt, and berries; blend until mixture is smooth. Pour into a tall glass.

---

**EACH SERVING:** ABOUT 230 CALORIES | 5G PROTEIN | 50G CARBOHYDRATE | 3G TOTAL FAT (0G SATURATED) | 5G FIBER | 0MG CHOLESTEROL | 25MG SODIUM

# BANANA–PEANUT BUTTER SMOOTHIE

For a thicker, colder smoothie, cut peeled banana into chunks and freeze up to one week in a zip-tight plastic bag.

---

**TOTAL TIME:** 5 MINUTES

**MAKES:** 1½ CUPS OR 1 SERVING

---

1   SMALL RIPE BANANA, CUT IN HALF

½   CUP SOY MILK

1   TEASPOON CREAMY PEANUT BUTTER

3   ICE CUBES

---

In blender, combine banana, soy milk, peanut butter, and ice cubes; blend until mixture is smooth and frothy. Pour into tall glass.

---

**EACH SERVING:** ABOUT 165 CALORIES | 6G PROTEIN | 28G CARBOHYDRATE | 4G TOTAL FAT (2G SATURATED) | 2G FIBER | 5MG CHOLESTEROL | 85MG SODIUM

# REDUCED-FAT GRANOLA

We baked oats, almonds, quinoa, wheat germ, and sesame seeds with apple juice instead of the usual oil and butter to create a vegan granola with just a fraction of the fat.

---

**ACTIVE TIME:** 10 MINUTES · **TOTAL TIME:** 35 MINUTES

**MAKES:** 6 CUPS OR 12 SERVINGS

---

4   CUPS OLD-FASHIONED OATS, UNCOOKED

½   CUP MAPLE SYRUP

½   CUP APPLE JUICE

1½  TEASPOONS VANILLA EXTRACT

¾   TEASPOON GROUND CINNAMON

½   CUP NATURAL ALMONDS

½   CUP QUINOA, THOROUGHLY RINSED

¼   CUP TOASTED WHEAT GERM

2   TABLESPOONS SESAME SEEDS

½   CUP DRIED APRICOTS, CUT INTO ¼-INCH PIECES

½   CUP DARK SEEDLESS RAISINS

---

**1**  Preheat oven to 350°F. Place oats in two 15½" by 10½" jelly-roll pans. Bake oats until lightly toasted, about 15 minutes, stirring twice.

**2**  In large bowl, with wire whisk, mix maple syrup, apple juice, vanilla, and cinnamon until blended. Add toasted oats, almonds, quinoa, wheat germ, and sesame seeds; stir well to coat.

**3**  Spread oat mixture evenly in same jelly-roll pans; bake until golden brown, 20 to 25 minutes, stirring frequently. Cool in pans on wire rack.

**4**  Transfer granola to large bowl; stir in apricots and raisins. Store at room temperature in tightly covered container up to 1 month.

---

**EACH SERVING:** ABOUT 350 CALORIES | 12G PROTEIN | 64G CARBOHYDRATE | 8G TOTAL FAT (2G SATURATED) | 8G FIBER | 0MG CHOLESTEROL | 10MG SODIUM

# GRANOLA-YOGURT PARFAIT

**A healthy breakfast doesn't get any easier (or more delicious) than this.**

TOTAL TIME: 5 MINUTES

MAKES: 1 SERVING

½ CUP FRESH OR FROZEN (PARTIALLY THAWED) RASPBERRIES OR OTHER FAVORITE BERRY

¾ CUP NONDAIRY VANILLA YOGURT

2 TABLESPOONS REDUCED-FAT GRANOLA (OPPOSITE)

Into parfait glass or wineglass, spoon some of the raspberries, nondairy yogurt, and granola. Repeat layering until all ingredients are used.

**EACH SERVING:** ABOUT 295 CALORIES | 8G PROTEIN | 70G CARBOHYDRATE | 21G TOTAL FAT (4G SATURATED) | 18G FIBER | 0MG CHOLESTEROL | 47MG SODIUM

# TOFU SCRAMBLE WITH CHOPPED TOMATOES AND CHIVES

Here's a tasty tofu scramble flecked with tomato and chives, and seasoned with garlic, turmeric, and a dash of lemon juice for zip.

**TOTAL TIME:** 15 MINUTES

**MAKES:** 4 SERVINGS

| | | | |
|---|---|---|---|
| 1 | PACKAGE (14 OUNCES) FIRM TOFU | | PINCH GROUND RED PEPPER (CAYENNE) |
| 3 | TABLESPOONS EXTRA-VIRGIN OLIVE OIL | ½ | TEASPOON TURMERIC |
| 1 | LARGE GARLIC CLOVE, FINELY CHOPPED | 1 | LARGE TOMATO, SEEDED AND CHOPPED |
| ¼ | CUP SNIPPED FRESH CHIVES | ½ | TEASPOON SALT |
| | | 1 | TABLESPOON LEMON JUICE |

1  Rinse tofu and press with clean towel to absorb excess water. Place in bowl and mash into small pieces with fork.

2  In nonstick 12-inch skillet, heat oil over medium heat until hot. Stir in garlic, chives, ground red pepper, and turmeric; cook for 2 minutes, stirring.

3  Add mashed tofu, tomato, and salt; raise heat and simmer 5 minutes. Remove from heat and stir in lemon juice.

**EACH SERVING:** ABOUT 190 CALORIES | 9G PROTEIN | 5G CARBOHYDRATE | 15G TOTAL FAT (2G SATURATED) | 2G FIBER | 0MG CHOLESTEROL | 297MG SODIUM

# SOUTH-OF-THE-BORDER VEGETABLE HASH

This savory combination of classic hash ingredients (minus the meat!) gets a new flavor twist from kidney beans, cilantro, and, if you choose, a squeeze of lime juice. Serve with fruit salad or a smoothie for a brunch that's as easy as it is satisfying.

**ACTIVE TIME:** 20 MINUTES · **TOTAL TIME:** 50 MINUTES

**MAKES:** 4 SERVINGS

3   LARGE YUKON GOLD POTATOES (1½ POUNDS), CUT INTO ¾-INCH PIECES

2   TABLESPOONS OLIVE OIL

1   LARGE ONION (12 OUNCES), CUT INTO ¼-INCH PIECES

1   MEDIUM RED PEPPER (4 TO 6 OUNCES), CUT INTO ¼-INCH-WIDE STRIPS

3   GARLIC CLOVES, CRUSHED WITH GARLIC PRESS

2   TEASPOONS GROUND CUMIN

¾   TEASPOON SALT

1   CAN (15 TO 19 OUNCES) RED KIDNEY OR BLACK BEANS, RINSED AND DRAINED, OR ½ CUP HOME-COOKED BEANS, PAGE 10

2   TABLESPOONS CHOPPED FRESH CILANTRO

**ACCOMPANIMENTS**
NONDAIRY PLAIN YOGURT, LIME WEDGES, SALSA, AND WARMED CORN TORTILLAS (OPTIONAL)

**1**   In 3-quart saucepan, place potatoes and enough water to cover; heat to boiling over high heat. Reduce heat to low; cover and simmer until potatoes are almost tender, about 5 minutes; drain well.

**2**   Meanwhile, in nonstick 12-inch skillet, heat oil over medium heat until hot. Add onion, red pepper, garlic, cumin, and salt; cook 10 minutes, stirring occasionally. Add drained potatoes and cook, turning them occasionally, until vegetables are lightly browned, about 5 minutes longer. Stir in beans and cook until heated through, 2 minutes longer. Sprinkle with cilantro.

**3**   Serve vegetable hash with yogurt, lime wedges, salsa, and tortillas, if you like.

**EACH SERVING:** ABOUT 360 CALORIES | 12G PROTEIN | 63G CARBOHYDRATE | 8G TOTAL FAT (1G SATURATED) | 13G FIBER | 0MG CHOLESTEROL | 625MG SODIUM

# 5-MINUTE MULTIGRAIN CEREAL

Get a great-grains start to your day with a hot, tasty serving of three kinds of grains in five minutes. Serve it with your choice of soy or rice milk.

**ACTIVE TIME:** 5 MINUTES · **TOTAL TIME:** 10 MINUTES
**MAKES:** 1 SERVING

- 2 TABLESPOONS QUICK-COOKING BARLEY
- 2 TABLESPOONS BULGUR
- 2 TABLESPOONS OLD-FASHIONED OATS, UNCOOKED
- ⅔ CUP WATER
- 2 TABLESPOONS RAISINS
- PINCH GROUND CINNAMON
- 1 TABLESPOON CHOPPED WALNUTS OR PECANS

In microwave-safe 1-quart bowl, combine barley, bulgur, oats, and water. Microwave on High 2 minutes. Stir in raisins and cinnamon; microwave 3 minutes longer. Stir, then top with walnuts.

**EACH SERVING:** ABOUT 265 CALORIES | 8G PROTEIN | 50G CARBOHYDRATE | 6G TOTAL FAT (1G SATURATED) | 7G FIBER | 0MG CHOLESTEROL | 5MG SODIUM

# VEGAN-WISE
## GUIDE TO NONDAIRY MILK

As more people reduce their dairy intake, milk substitutions multiply. Now there's a wide assortment of products to choose from. Found in the refrigerator section of the grocery store and in shelf-stable cartons, these beverages come plain or flavored, organic or not, with different degrees of enrichment.

**Soy milk:** A good substitute for cow's milk in any almost any recipe, in a bowl of breakfast cereal, or by the glassful, this creamy nondairy beverage is made by pressing cooked ground soybeans. It is higher in protein than cow's milk, lower in fat, and contains no cholesterol. However, it is also low in calcium, so consider purchasing a fortified version. Flavor varies considerably from brand to brand, so experiment until you find one you like. Unsweetened soy milk is useful for baking.

**Almond milk:** This nut milk has a creamy consistency similar to soy milk and a delicate, slightly sweet flavor that's delicious in smoothies and desserts or for drinking. Almonds are one of the healthiest nuts you can eat, so why not enjoy the benefits in a beverage? Take note that the amount of almonds per cup is small though—almonds are expensive!—so you should check the label for additives and sweeteners in the milk.

**Rice milk:** Many people who don't like the flavor or consistency of soy milk appreciate this light, slightly sweet milk substitute made by converting rice into a sweetener and then into a beverage. Although tasty, it is less nutritious than soy or almond milk. Because of this, some brands are selling a combination soy-rice milk. Rice milk is delicious in desserts; look for it frozen as an ice cream substitute.

**Coconut milk beverage:** A sweet and creamy coconut milk product is now available in grocery and health-food stores. The makers have reduced the fat and richness of pure coconut milk to create a multi-purpose nondairy beverage that anyone who loves coconut milk will embrace. When cooking curries or baking desserts, diluted canned coconut milk is still usually the best choice, but this beverage is a great-tasting option to sip from a glass, pour over cereal, or whip out of the fridge when you need a whole-milk alternative.

# WHOLE-GRAIN CARROT CAKE MUFFINS

These muffins are as scrumptious as carrot cake, but contain good-for-you grains so you can indulge without guilt.

**ACTIVE TIME:** 20 MINUTES · **TOTAL TIME:** 45 MINUTES

**MAKES:** 12 MUFFINS

| | |
|---|---|
| 1 CUP QUICK-COOKING OATS | 1¼ CUPS PLAIN UNSWEETENED SOY MILK |
| 1 CUP ALL-PURPOSE FLOUR | ¼ CUP UNSWEETENED APPLESAUCE |
| ½ CUP WHOLE-WHEAT FLOUR | 3 TABLESPOONS CANOLA OIL |
| ½ CUP PACKED BROWN SUGAR | 1 TEASPOON VANILLA EXTRACT |
| 2 TEASPOONS BAKING POWDER | 2 CUPS SHREDDED CARROTS |
| ½ TEASPOON BAKING SODA | ½ CUP RAISINS |
| ½ TEASPOON SALT | 1 TEASPOON GRANULATED SUGAR |
| 1 TEASPOON PUMPKIN PIE SPICE | |

**1** Preheat oven to 400°F. Grease muffin tin with nonstick cooking spray.

**2** Place oats in blender and blend until finely ground.

**3** In large bowl, combine oats, all-purpose and whole-wheat flours, brown sugar, baking powder, baking soda, salt, and pumpkin pie spice. In small bowl, with fork, blend soy milk, applesauce, oil, and vanilla. Stir into flour mixture until flour is moistened. Fold in carrots and raisins.

**4** Spoon batter into muffin-pan cups (cups will be very full). Sprinkle with granulated sugar. Bake 23 to 27 minutes or until toothpick inserted in center of muffins comes out clean. Remove to wire rack; serve warm, or cool to serve later.

**EACH SERVING:** ABOUT 190 CALORIES | 4G PROTEIN | 35G CARBOHYDRATE | 5G TOTAL FAT (0.5G SATURATED) | 3G FIBER | 0MG CHOLESTEROL | 270MG SODIUM

# BLUEBERRY MUFFINS

When retooling a recipe to be egg-free, oil and/or fruit purees are often used to provide the moistness eggs typically supply. In this recipe, applesauce plays that role.

---

ACTIVE TIME: 20 MINUTES · TOTAL TIME: 45 MINUTES
MAKES: 12 MUFFINS

---

| | |
|---|---|
| 1 CUP QUICK-COOKING OATS | 1¼ CUPS PLAIN UNSWEETENED SOY MILK |
| 1 CUP ALL-PURPOSE FLOUR | ¼ CUP UNSWEETENED APPLESAUCE |
| ½ CUP WHOLE-WHEAT FLOUR | 3 TABLESPOONS CANOLA OIL |
| ½ CUP PACKED BROWN SUGAR | 1 TEASPOON VANILLA EXTRACT |
| 2 TEASPOONS BAKING POWDER | 2 CUPS BLUEBERRIES (SEE TIP) |
| ½ TEASPOON BAKING SODA | 1 TEASPOON GRANULATED SUGAR |
| ½ TEASPOON SALT | |

1  Preheat oven to 400°F. Line 12-cup muffin pan with paper liners.

2  Place oats in blender and blend until finely ground.

3  In large bowl, combine oats, all-purpose and whole-wheat flours, brown sugar, baking powder, baking soda, and salt. In small bowl, with fork, blend soy milk, applesauce, oil, and vanilla; stir into flour mixture until flour is moistened. Fold in blueberries.

4  Spoon batter into muffin-pan cups (cups will be very full). Sprinkle with granulated sugar. Bake until toothpick inserted in center of muffins comes out clean, 23 to 25 minutes. Remove to wire rack; serve warm, or cool to serve later.

TIP  If it's not blueberry season, feel free to substitute frozen blueberries. Just add 3 to 5 minutes to your baking time, as the frozen berries will lower the temperature of your batter from the get-go. A few blueberry streaks will make your muffins look homemade, but don't thaw the berries before adding them to the batter or you'll end up with a big purple mess.

---

EACH SERVING: ABOUT 80 CALORIES | 4G PROTEIN | 31G CARBOHYDRATE | 5G TOTAL FAT (0.5G SATURATED) | 2G FIBER | 0MG CHOLESTEROL | 254MG SODIUM

# WHOLE-GRAIN PANCAKES

These pancakes not only allow you to go egg-free, they give you a double dose of whole-grain goodness (notice the whole-wheat flour and heart-healthy oats in the ingredients list). Top with fresh seasonal fruit, maple syrup, or check out our Delicious Pancake Toppers, opposite.

**ACTIVE TIME:** 15 MINUTES · **TOTAL TIME:** 30 MINUTES

**MAKES:** 12 PANCAKES OR 4 SERVINGS

| | |
|---|---|
| 1½ CUPS PLAIN SOY MILK | 2 TEASPOONS BAKING POWDER |
| ⅔ CUP QUICK-COOKING OATS | ¼ TEASPOON SALT |
| ½ CUP ALL-PURPOSE FLOUR | 3 TABLESPOONS CANOLA OIL |
| ½ CUP WHOLE-WHEAT FLOUR | |

**1** In medium bowl, combine soy milk and oats. Let stand 10 minutes.

**2** Meanwhile, in a large bowl, combine all-purpose and whole-wheat flours, baking powder, and salt. Stir oil into oat mixture and add oat mixture to dry ingredients. Stir just until flour mixture is moistened (batter will be lumpy).

**3** Spray nonstick 12-inch skillet with nonstick cooking spray; heat over medium heat until hot. Making 4 pancakes at a time, pour batter by scant ¼ cups into skillet, spreading batter into 3½-inch circles. Cook until tops are bubbly and edges look dry, 2 to 3 minutes. With a wide spatula, turn pancakes and cook until undersides are golden brown. Transfer pancakes to platter. Cover to keep warm.

**4** Repeat with remaining batter, using more cooking spray as needed.

**EACH SERVING:** ABOUT 300 CALORIES | 8G PROTEIN | 37G CARBOHYDRATE | 14G TOTAL FAT (1G SATURATED) | 4G FIBER | 0MG CHOLESTEROL | 466MG SODIUM

# EASY VEGAN CONDIMENTS
## DELICIOUS PANCAKE TOPPERS

Maple syrup will always be a classic, but to keep things interesting, try these yummy nondairy toppings.

• Fresh seasonal fruit, like the raspberries and chopped nectarines shown in the photo above, drizzled with nondairy vanilla yogurt.

• Toasted nuts (walnuts, pecans, whatever you have on hand), sweetened coconut flakes, and maple syrup. Or, for a decadent treat, swap melted dark chocolate for the maple syrup (for tips on buying vegan chocolate, see page 149).

• Dollops of homemade Almond Ricotta (see recipe, page 119) plus fresh orange wedges.

# PECAN WAFFLES

Crisp on the outside and fluffy on the inside, these pecan-studded waffles will wow your brunch guests. Maple syrup and pecans are a delectable match, so don't skimp.

**ACTIVE TIME:** 10 MINUTES · **TOTAL TIME:** 20 MINUTES
**MAKES:** 6 WAFFLES

1¾ CUPS PLAIN UNSWEETENED SOY MILK

1 TEASPOON VANILLA EXTRACT

2 TABLESPOONS BROWN SUGAR

⅔ CUP QUICK-COOKING OATS

½ CUP ALL-PURPOSE FLOUR

½ CUP WHOLE-WHEAT FLOUR

2 TEASPOONS BAKING POWDER

¼ TEASPOON SALT

¼ CUP VEGETABLE OIL

½ CUP PECANS, TOASTED AND VERY FINELY CHOPPED

FRESH FRUIT OR MAPLE SYRUP (OPTIONAL)

1  In medium bowl, combine soy milk, vanilla, brown sugar, and oats. Let stand for 10 minutes.

2  Meanwhile, in large bowl, combine all-purpose and whole-wheat flours, baking powder, salt, and pecans. Stir oil into oat mixture and add to dry ingredients. Stir just until flour mixture is moistened (batter will be lumpy).

3  Spray a waffle iron with nonstick cooking spray and preheat. Spoon batter into waffle iron (amount will depend on waffle iron used) and cook according to manufacturer's directions until browned and crisp. When waffle is done, lift cover and loosen waffle with fork. Serve immediately with fresh fruit or maple syrup, if desired, or keep warm in oven (place waffles directly on oven rack in 250°F oven to keep crisp). Serve while hot and repeat with remaining batter.

**EACH SERVING:** ABOUT 225 CALORIES | 7G PROTEIN | 31G CARBOHYDRATE | 9G TOTAL FAT (1G SATURATED) | 4G FIBER | 0MG CHOLESTEROL | 317MG SODIUM

# PUMPKIN WAFFLES

These warmly spiced waffles are the perfect choice for brunch on a crisp fall day.

---

ACTIVE TIME: 15 MINUTES · TOTAL TIME: 45 MINUTES
MAKES: 18 (4-INCH) WAFFLES OR 9 SERVINGS

---

⅓  CUP QUICK-COOKING OATS

1½ CUPS ALL-PURPOSE FLOUR

1  CUP WHOLE-WHEAT FLOUR

¼  CUP PACKED BROWN SUGAR

1  TABLESPOON BAKING POWDER

1  TEASPOON PUMPKIN PIE SPICE

¾  TEASPOON BAKING SODA

½  TEASPOON SALT

2  CUPS PLAIN UNSWEETENED SOY MILK

1  CAN (15 OUNCES) SOLID PACK PUMPKIN (NOT PUMPKIN-PIE MIX)

¼  CUP CANOLA OIL

1  TEASPOON VANILLA EXTRACT

1  Place oats in blender and blend until finely ground. In a large bowl, mix oats, all-purpose and whole-wheat flours, brown sugar, baking powder, pumpkin pie spice, baking soda, and salt, breaking up any lumps of brown sugar.

2  In a medium bowl, stir together soy milk, oil, and vanilla until smooth. Add to dry ingredients and stir just until blended.

3  Spray a waffle iron with nonstick cooking spray and preheat. Spoon batter into waffle iron (amount will depend on waffle iron used) and cook according to manufacturer's directions until browned and crisp. When waffle is done, lift cover and loosen waffle with fork. Serve immediately with fresh fruit or maple syrup, if desired, or keep warm in oven (place waffles directly on oven rack in 250°F oven to keep crisp). Serve while hot and repeat with remaining batter.

---

**EACH SERVING:** ABOUT 385 CALORIES | 10G PROTEIN | 60G CARBOHYDRATE |12G TOTAL FAT (1G SATURATED) | 6G FIBER | 0MG CHOLESTEROL | 675MG SODIUM

# SATISFYING SANDWICHES

In this chapter, we've provided lots of tempting sandwich ideas, including some fun vegan riffs on classics, like Tempeh Reubens with home-made Thousand Island Dressing and Souvlaki Sandwiches made from store-bought veggie burgers. And, speaking of burgers, we include two meat-free versions here and additional options in the Great Grilling chapter, page 81. You'll see that satisfyingly "meaty" burgers can be made from bulgur and black beans or Portobello mushroom caps.

These recipes also offer lots of opportunities to incorporate whole-grain goodness into your lunch hour. Serve the Health Club Sandwich on multigrain toast, or choose a whole-wheat pita instead of white when you make pita pizzas or falafel. If a sandwich just isn't a sandwich without mayonnaise, try our yummy tofu-based recipes for mayo and aïoli. It will also come in handy when it's time to make our splendid Eggless Egg Salad Sandwich (which substitutes tofu and turmeric for the eggs, by the way!).

*Whole-Wheat Pita Pizzas (page 47)*

# FALAFEL SANDWICHES

Serve these small Middle-Eastern bean patties in pita pockets with lettuce, tomatoes, cucumbers, and tangy nondairy yogurt.

**ACTIVE TIME:** 10 MINUTES · **TOTAL TIME:** 25 MINUTES

**MAKES:** 4 SANDWICHES

4  GREEN ONIONS, CUT INTO ½-INCH PIECES

2  GARLIC CLOVES, EACH CUT IN HALF

½  CUP PACKED FRESH ITALIAN PARSLEY LEAVES

2  TEASPOONS DRIED MINT

1  CAN (15 TO 19 OUNCES) GARBANZO BEANS, RINSED AND DRAINED

½  CUP PLAIN DRIED BREAD CRUMBS

1  TEASPOON GROUND CORIANDER

1  TEASPOON GROUND CUMIN

1  TEASPOON BAKING POWDER

½  TEASPOON SALT

¼  TEASPOON GROUND RED PEPPER (CAYENNE)

¼  TEASPOON GROUND ALLSPICE

OLIVE OIL NONSTICK COOKING SPRAY

4  (6- TO 7-INCH) WHOLE-WHEAT PITA BREADS

**ACCOMPANIMENTS**

SLICED ROMAINE LETTUCE, SLICED RIPE TOMATOES, SLICED CUCUMBER, SLICED RED ONION, NONDAIRY PLAIN YOGURT (OPTIONAL)

**1**  In food processor with knife blade attached, finely chop green onions, garlic, parsley leaves, and mint. Add beans, bread crumbs, coriander, cumin, baking powder, salt, ground red pepper, and allspice; blend until a coarse puree forms.

**2**  With hands, shape bean mixture, by scant ½ cups, into eight 3-inch round patties and place on sheet of waxed paper. Coat both sides of patties with cooking spray.

**3**  Heat nonstick 10-inch skillet on medium-high until hot. Add half of patties and cook until dark golden brown, about 8 minutes, turning them over once. Transfer patties to paper towels to drain. Repeat with remaining patties.

**4**  Cut off top third of each pita to form a pocket. Place two warm patties in each pita. Serve with choice of accompaniments.

**EACH SANDWICH WITHOUT ACCOMPANIMENTS:** ABOUT 365 CALORIES | 14G PROTEIN 68G CARBOHYDRATE | 5G TOTAL FAT (1G SATURATED) | 10G FIBER | 5MG CHOLESTEROL 1,015MG SODIUM

# BBQ TOFU SANDWICHES

**If you're craving barbecue, try this quick and easy tofu version.**

**ACTIVE TIME:** 20 MINUTES · **TOTAL TIME:** 25 MINUTES

**MAKES:** 4 SANDWICHES

| | |
|---|---|
| 1 PACKAGE (16 OUNCES) EXTRA-FIRM TOFU | ⅛ TEASPOON GROUND RED PEPPER (CAYENNE) |
| ¼ CUP KETCHUP | 2 GARLIC CLOVES, CRUSHED WITH GARLIC PRESS |
| 2 TABLESPOONS DIJON MUSTARD | 2 TEASPOONS SESAME SEEDS |
| 2 TABLESPOONS REDUCED-SODIUM SOY SAUCE | 8 SLICES WHOLE-GRAIN BREAD, TOASTED |
| 1 TABLESPOON MOLASSES | |
| 1 TABLESPOON GRATED, PEELED FRESH GINGER | **ACCOMPANIMENTS** SLICED RIPE TOMATOES, SLICED RED ONION, AND LETTUCE LEAVES (OPTIONAL) |

**1** Drain tofu; wrap in clean dish towel. Place wrapped tofu in pie plate; top with a dinner plate. Place 1 or 2 heavy cans on top of plate to weight down tofu to extract excess water; set aside about 15 minutes.

**2** Meanwhile, preheat broiler. Coat rack in broiling pan with nonstick cooking spray.

**3** In small bowl, combine ketchup, mustard, soy sauce, molasses, ginger, ground red pepper, and garlic, stirring until blended.

**4** Remove plate and cans, unwrap tofu, and discard water in pie plate. Place tofu on cutting board with shorter side facing you. Cut tofu length-wise into 8 slices.

**5** Place slices on rack in broiling pan; brush with half of ketchup mixture. Place in broiler about 5 inches from source of heat and broil tofu until ketchup mixture looks dry, about 3 minutes. With metal spatula, turn slices over; brush with remaining ketchup mixture and sprinkle with sesame seeds. Broil tofu 3 minutes longer.

**6** To serve, place 2 tofu slices on 1 slice of toasted bread. Top with tomato, onion, and lettuce, if you like. Top with another slice of bread. Repeat with remaining tofu and bread.

**EACH SANDWICH WITHOUT ACCOMPANIMENTS:** ABOUT 230 CALORIES | 14G PROTEIN 35G CARBOHYDRATE | 55G TOTAL FAT | (0G SATURATED) | 2G FIBER | 0MG CHOLESTEROL 975 MG SODIUM

# HEALTH CLUB SANDWICHES

This carrot, sprout, and bean spread combo will delight your palate and satisfy your hunger. To make it extra wholesome, we suggest using multigrain toast, but sourdough bread would be delicious, too.

**TOTAL TIME:** 25 MINUTES

**MAKES:** 4 SANDWICHES

2   TABLESPOONS OLIVE OIL

2   TEASPOONS PLUS 1 TABLESPOON FRESH LEMON JUICE

1   TEASPOON HONEY OR AGAVE NECTAR (SEE TIP)

⅛   TEASPOON GROUND BLACK PEPPER

3   CARROTS, PEELED AND SHREDDED (1 CUP)

2   CUPS ALFALFA SPROUTS

1   GARLIC CLOVE, FINELY CHOPPED

½   TEASPOON GROUND CUMIN

PINCH GROUND RED PEPPER (CAYENNE)

1   CAN (15 TO 19 OUNCES) GARBANZO BEANS, RINSED AND DRAINED

1   TABLESPOON WATER

8   SLICES MULTIGRAIN BREAD, LIGHTLY TOASTED

1   LARGE RIPE TOMATO (10 TO 12 OUNCES), THINLY SLICED

1   BUNCH (4 OUNCES) WATERCRESS, TOUGH STEMS TRIMMED

**1**  In medium bowl, stir 1 tablespoon oil, 2 teaspoons lemon juice, honey or agave nectar, and ground black pepper until mixed. Add carrots and alfalfa sprouts; toss until mixed and evenly coated with dressing.

**2**  In 2-quart saucepan, heat remaining 1 tablespoon oil over medium heat. Add garlic, cumin, and ground red pepper and cook until very fragrant. Stir in garbanzo beans and remove from heat. Add remaining 1 tablespoon lemon juice and water; mash to a coarse puree.

**3**  Spread bean mixture on 8 toast slices. Place tomato slices and watercress over 4 slices. Top with alfalfa-sprout mixture. Cover with 4 remaining toast slices, placing garbanzo-topped sides onto filling.

**TIP**  Many vegans consider honey off-limits because it is a byproduct of bees (just as milk is a byproduct of cows). Agave nectar is a natural sweetener derived from cactuses that's a great substitute.

**EACH SANDWICH:** ABOUT 380 CALORIES | 14G PROTEIN | 57G CARBOHYDRATE | 12G TOTAL FAT (2G SATURATED) | 17G FIBER | 0MG CHOLESTEROL | 545MG SODIUM

# EGGLESS EGG SALAD SANDWICHES

Tofu plays a key role in this faux egg salad, absorbing the flavorings and providing the egg-like creaminess. Turmeric contributes its "egg yolk" yellow. You can use store-bought soy mayonnaise, or try our easy recipe for vegan mayonnaise made from silken tofu, opposite.

**TOTAL TIME:** 15 MINUTES PLUS CHILLING

**MAKES:** 4 SERVINGS

| | |
|---|---|
| 1 PACKAGE (16 OUNCES) FIRM TOFU, DRAINED | ½ TEASPOON TURMERIC |
| ¼ CUP SOY MAYONNAISE (SEE PAGE 39 TO MAKE YOUR OWN) | 2 SMALL STALKS CELERY, THINLY SLICED |
| 1 TABLESPOON SWEET PICKLE RELISH | 8 SLICES WHOLE-GRAIN BREAD |
| 2 TEASPOONS SOY MILK | 1 HEAD BOSTON LETTUCE |
| ¾ TEASPOON DIJON MUSTARD | 2 SMALL RIPE TOMATOES (4 OUNCES EACH), SLICED |
| ½ TEASPOON SALT | |

**1** In medium bowl, with fork, mix tofu with mayonnaise, pickle relish, soy milk, mustard, salt, and turmeric until tofu breaks down into small pieces the size of peas. Stir in celery. Cover and refrigerate to allow flavors to blend or until ready to serve.

**2** To serve, top 4 bread slices with tofu mixture, arrange lettuce leaves and tomato slices on top; cover with remaining bread slices.

**EACH SERVING:** ABOUT 305 CALORIES | 19G PROTEIN | 31G CARBOHYDRATE | 12G TOTAL FAT (2G SATURATED) | 6G FIBER | 0MG CHOLESTEROL | 696MG SODIUM

## EASY VEGAN CONDIMENTS
# VEGAN MAYONNAISE

**You don't have to give up mayo to go vegan. Here's a basic foolproof recipe plus two flavorful variations.**

**TOTAL TIME:** 2 MINUTES
**MAKES:** ¾ CUP

½ CUP SILKEN TOFU
½ TEASPOON DIJON MUSTARD
2 TEASPOONS CIDER VINEGAR
¼ TEASPOON SALT
1 TABLESPOON PLUS 2 TEASPOONS CANOLA OIL

**1** Combine tofu, mustard, vinegar, and salt in blender; blend until completely smooth.
**2** Through hole in top of blender, slowly add oil, blending until completely combined.

## AÏOLI

Add **1 garlic clove**, crushed with a garlic press, in Step 1.

## HERB MAYONNAISE

Add **1 tablespoon chopped fresh herbs** in Step 1.

**EACH SERVING**: ABOUT 20 CALORIES | 0.5G PROTEIN | 0G CARBOHYDRATE | 2G TOTAL FAT (0G SATURATED | 0G FIBER | 0MG CHOLESTEROL | 53MG SODIUM

# TEMPEH REUBEN SANDWICH

Here seasoned strips of crispy tempeh (and a luscious soy mayonnaise-based dressing) stand in for the corned beef and famous sauce of the original. The end result: complete satisfaction!

**ACTIVE TIME:** 10 MINUTES · **TOTAL TIME:** 35 MINUTES

**MAKES:** 4 SANDWICHES

| | |
|---|---|
| 1 PACKAGE (8 OUNCES) TEMPEH, CUT CROSSWISE TO MAKE 4 SQUARES | 1 TEASPOON COARSELY GROUND BLACK PEPPER |
| 2 GARLIC CLOVES | 1 CUP SAUERKRAUT, DRAINED WELL |
| 2 CUPS VEGETABLE BROTH | 1 RIPE AVOCADO |
| 1 BAY LEAF | 3 TABLESPOONS CANOLA OIL |
| 1 TEASPOON GROUND CORIANDER | 8 SLICES RYE BREAD |
| 1 TEASPOON PAPRIKA | ¼ CUP THOUSAND ISLAND DRESSING (SEE RECIPE OPPOSITE) |
| ½ TEASPOON GROUND GINGER | |

**1** In medium saucepan, heat tempeh, garlic, broth, and bay leaf to boiling over high heat. Reduce heat to low; cover and simmer for 25 minutes, turning once. Remove tempeh from liquid and cool. Discard liquid, garlic, and bay leaf. Cut each square of tempeh horizontally in half and toss in bowl with coriander, paprika, ginger, and pepper.

**2** In small bowl, mash avocado.

**3** In nonstick 12-inch skillet, heat oil over medium-high heat until hot. Add tempeh and cook until browned and crisped, about 7 minutes, turning once.

**4** Meanwhile, toast bread. Spread mashed avocado onto 4 slices toasted bread. Top each avocado-covered slice with 2 pieces tempeh and 3 tablespoons sauerkraut. Spread 1 tablespoon dressing onto remaining 4 slices and place on top of tempeh slices. Cut in half and serve.

**EACH SERVING:** ABOUT 465 CALORIES | 19G PROTEIN | 47G CARBOHYDRATE | 24G TOTAL FAT (3G SATURATED) | 12G FIBER | 0MG CHOLESTEROL | 773MG SODIUM

# THOUSAND ISLAND DRESSING

**After you flavor your Reuben with this creamy sauce, save the extra for salad dressing or as a tasty topper for tofu dogs or veggie burgers.**

**TOTAL TIME:** 3 MINUTES

**MAKES:** ¾ CUP OR 12 SERVINGS

½ CUP SOY MAYONNAISE (SEE PAGE 39 TO MAKE YOUR OWN)

3 TABLESPOONS KETCHUP

3 TEASPOONS WHITE WINE VINEGAR

2 TEASPOONS AGAVE SYRUP (SEE TIP, PAGE 36)

¼ TEASPOON ONION POWDER

4 TEASPOONS SWEET PICKLE RELISH

PINCH SALT AND GROUND BLACK PEPPER

**1** Combine tofu, mustard, vinegar, and salt in blender; blend until completely smooth.

**2** Through hole in top of blender, slowly add oil, blending until completely combined.

**EACH SERVING:** ABOUT 40 CALORIES | 1G PROTEIN | 3G CARBOHYDRATE | 3G TOTAL FAT (0.5G SATURATED) | 0G FIBER | 0MG CHOLESTEROL | 145MG SODIUM

# BULGUR BEAN BURGERS

Why buy expensive veggie burgers in the store when they're so easy to make at home? This version gets its "meaty" texture from bulgur and black beans. A mint-and-cucumber yogurt sauce (nondairy, of course!) make these burgers guest worthy.

**ACTIVE TIME:** 20 MINUTES · **TOTAL TIME:** 28 MINUTES

**MAKES:** 4 BURGERS

1   CUP WATER

¾   TEASPOON SALT

½   CUP BULGUR

1   CAN (15 TO 19 OUNCES) REDUCED-SODIUM BLACK BEANS, RINSED AND DRAINED, OR 1½ CUPS HOME-COOKED BEANS, PAGE 10

1   CONTAINER (6 OUNCES) NONDAIRY PLAIN YOGURT

¼   TEASPOON GROUND ALLSPICE

¼   TEASPOON GROUND CINNAMON

¼   TEASPOON GROUND CUMIN

¼   CUP PACKED FRESH MINT LEAVES, CHOPPED

NONSTICK COOKING SPRAY

⅛   TEASPOON GROUND BLACK PEPPER

½   CUP SHREDDED KIRBY (PICKLING) CUCUMBER (1 SMALL)

4   LETTUCE LEAVES

1   RIPE MEDIUM TOMATO (6 TO 8 OUNCES), SLICED

4   WHOLE-WHEAT HAMBURGER BUNS

**1**   In 1-quart saucepan, heat water and ½ teaspoon salt to boiling over high heat. Stir in bulgur. Reduce heat to low; cover and simmer until water is absorbed, 10 to 12 minutes.

**2**   Meanwhile, in large bowl, with potato masher or fork, mash beans with 2 tablespoons yogurt until almost smooth. Stir in bulgur, allspice, cinnamon, cumin, and half of mint until combined. With lightly floured hands, shape bean mixture into four 3-inch round patties. Coat both sides of each patty lightly with cooking spray.

**3**   Heat nonstick 12-inch skillet over medium heat until hot. Add burgers and cook until lightly browned and heated through, about 8 minutes, turning them over once.

**4**   While burgers are cooking, prepare yogurt sauce: In small bowl, combine the cucumber, remaining yogurt, remaining mint, remaining ¼ teaspoon salt, and pepper. Makes about 1¼ cups.

**5**   Divide lettuce, tomato slices, and burgers on bottom halves of buns; add some yogurt sauce and top halves of buns. Serve with remaining yogurt sauce on the side.

**EACH BURGER:** ABOUT 355 CALORIES | 16G PROTEIN | 66G CARBOHYDRATE | 4G TOTAL FAT (0.5G SATURATED) | 15G FIBER | 0MG CHOLESTEROL | 738MG SODIUM

# VEGAN BURGERS WITH AVOCADO SALSA

It's the toppings that make these burgers—start with store-bought vegan soy burgers (or make our Bulgur Bean Burgers, page 43), then turn them into something special with avocado, tomato, lettuce, and alfalfa sprouts.

**TOTAL TIME:** 30 MINUTES

**MAKES:** 4 BURGERS

| | |
|---|---|
| 1 RIPE MEDIUM AVOCADO | 2 PACKAGES (6.35 OUNCES EACH, 4 BURGERS TOTAL) REFRIGERATED VEGAN SOY BURGERS |
| 1 GREEN ONION, CHOPPED | |
| 2 TABLESPOONS BOTTLED MILD SALSA | 4 SANDWICH ROLLS, SPLIT |
| 1 TEASPOON FRESH LEMON JUICE | 1 LARGE RIPE TOMATO (10 TO 12 OUNCES) |
| 1 TABLESPOON CHOPPED FRESH CILANTRO | 4 LARGE LETTUCE LEAVES |
| ¼ TEASPOON SALT | 1 CUP ALFALFA SPROUTS |

**1** Preheat broiler.

**2** Cut avocado lengthwise in half; remove seed and peel. In small bowl, mash avocado; stir in green onion, salsa, lemon juice, cilantro, and salt.

**3** Prepare soy burgers as label directs. Meanwhile, toast sandwich rolls and slice tomato.

**4** On 4 dinner plates, arrange lettuce leaves on bottom halves of toasted rolls; top with tomato slices, burgers, and avocado mixture. Replace tops. Serve with alfalfa sprouts.

**EACH BURGER:** ABOUT 330 CALORIES | 19G PROTEIN | 40G CARBOHYDRATE | 12G TOTAL FAT (2G SATURATED) | 11G FIBER | 0MG CHOLESTEROL | 738MG SODIUM

# ZUCCHINI AND BEAN BURRITOS

Here's a quick dairy-free version of the sort of burritos restaurants serve. Warm broccoli and carrot slaw makes a great side dish (see recipe, page 51).

**ACTIVE TIME:** 15 MINUTES · **TOTAL TIME:** 25 MINUTES
**MAKES:** 4 MAIN-DISH SERVINGS

2   TEASPOONS VEGETABLE OIL

4   MEDIUM ZUCCHINI (ABOUT 5 OUNCES EACH), EACH CUT LENGTHWISE IN HALF, THEN SLICED CROSSWISE

¼   TEASPOONS SALT

¼   TEASPOON GROUND CINNAMON

1   CAN (15 OUNCES) SPANISH-STYLE RED KIDNEY BEANS

1   CAN (15 TO 19 OUNCES) BLACK BEANS, RINSED AND DRAINED

4   FLOUR TORTILLAS, 10 INCHES EACH

1   CUP SHREDDED NONDAIRY MONTEREY JACK CHEESE (OPTIONAL)

½   CUP LOOSELY PACKED FRESH CILANTRO LEAVES

1   JAR (16-OUNCES) CHUNKY-STYLE SALSA

**1** In 12-inch skillet, heat oil over medium-high heat. Add zucchini, salt, and cinnamon; cook until zucchini is tender-crisp, about 5 minutes.
**2** Meanwhile, in 2-quart saucepan, heat kidney beans with their sauce and black beans over medium heat just to simmering; keep warm.
**3** Microwave tortillas on a plate between paper towels on High for 1 to 2 minutes or until heated through. Allow each person to assemble burrito as desired, using a warm flour tortilla, zucchini, bean mixture, cheese, if using, and cilantro leaves. Pass salsa to serve with burritos.

**EACH SERVING:** ABOUT 480 CALORIES | 19G PROTEIN | 80G CARBOHYDRATE | 10G TOTAL FAT (2G SATURATED) | 20G FIBER | 0MG CHOLESTEROL | 953MG SODIUM

# SOUVLAKI SANDWICHES

**No one will miss the meat in these yummy sandwiches. Make the filling by cutting up your favorite veggie burgers. Top with a refreshing nondairy yogurt sauce seasoned with cucumbers, mint, and garlic.**

**ACTIVE TIME:** 20 MINUTES · **TOTAL TIME:** 25 MINUTES

**MAKES:** 4 SANDWICHES

| | | | |
|---|---|---|---|
| 1 | TABLESPOON OLIVE OIL | 1 | ENGLISH (SEEDLESS) CUCUMBER (8 OUNCES), CUT INTO ¼-INCH PIECES (SEE TIP) |
| 1 | LARGE ONION (12 OUNCES), CUT IN HALF AND THINLY SLICED | | |
| 4 | FROZEN VEGAN SOY BURGERS (10- TO 12-OUNCE PACKAGE), CUT INTO 1-INCH PIECES | 1 | TEASPOON DRIED MINT |
| | | 1 | SMALL GARLIC CLOVE, CRUSHED WITH GARLIC PRESS |
| ¼ | TEASPOON GROUND BLACK PEPPER | 4 | (6- TO 7-INCH) PITA BREADS, WARMED |
| ½ | TEASPOON SALT | 1 | RIPE MEDIUM TOMATO (6 TO 8 OUNCES), CUT INTO ½-INCH PIECES |
| 1 | CUP (8 OUNCES) NONDAIRY PLAIN YOGURT | 1 | OUNCE NONDAIRY FETA CHEESE, CRUMBLED (¼ CUP; OPTIONAL) |

**1** In nonstick 12-inch skillet, heat oil over medium heat until hot. Add onion and cook until tender and golden, 12 to 15 minutes, stirring occasionally. Add burger pieces, pepper, and ¼ teaspoon salt; cook until heated through, about 5 minutes.

**2** Meanwhile, in medium bowl, stir yogurt with cucumber, mint, garlic, and remaining ¼ teaspoon salt. Add burger mixture and toss gently to combine.

**3** Cut 1-inch slice from each pita to make opening. Reserve cut-off pitas for crumbs another day. Spoon one-fourth of burger mixture into each pita. Sprinkle with tomato and feta.

**TIP** If a recipe calls for an English cucumber and you use a classic cuke with a waxed skin, peel it and discard the seeds if they're bitter. Cut the cucumber in half lengthwise, then using a teaspoon, scoop out the center by scraping down the length.

**EACH SANDWICH:** ABOUT 335 CALORIES | 21G PROTEIN | 52G CARBOHYDRATE | 6G TOTAL FAT (1G SATURATED) | 7G FIBER | 0MG CHOLESTEROL | 953MG SODIUM

# WHOLE-WHEAT PITA PIZZAS

We topped whole-wheat pitas with vegan ricotta cheese (see page 119 for the simple recipe, made from almonds!), garbanzo beans, and sautéed vegetables for a fast dinner the whole family will love. For photo, see page 32.

**ACTIVE TIME:** 25 MINUTES · **TOTAL TIME:** 35 MINUTES

**MAKES:** 4 MAIN-DISH SERVINGS

1   TEASPOON OLIVE OIL

1   MEDIUM RED ONION, SLICED

2   GARLIC CLOVES, CRUSHED WITH GARLIC PRESS

¼   TEASPOON CRUSHED RED PEPPER

8   OUNCES BROCCOLI FLOWERETS (HALF 16-OUNCE BAG), CUT INTO 1½-INCH PIECES

½   TEASPOON SALT

¼   CUP WATER

1   CAN (15 TO 19 OUNCES) GARBANZO BEANS, RINSED AND DRAINED

1   CUP ALMOND RICOTTA (PAGE 119)

4   (6-INCH) WHOLE-WHEAT PITA BREADS, SPLIT HORIZONTALLY IN HALF

½   CUP GRATED NONDAIRY PARMESAN SEASONING

2   RIPE MEDIUM PLUM TOMATOES, CUT INTO ½-INCH PIECES

**1**   Preheat oven to 450°F.

**2**   In nonstick 12-inch skillet, heat oil over medium heat until hot. Add onion and cook until golden, 8 to 10 minutes, stirring occasionally. Add garlic and crushed red pepper; cook 30 seconds, stirring. Add broccoli, ¼ teaspoon salt, and water; heat to boiling. Cover and cook until broccoli is tender-crisp, about 5 minutes.

**3**   Meanwhile, in small bowl, with potato masher or fork, mash garbanzo beans with Almond Ricotta and remaining ¼ teaspoon salt until almost smooth.

**4**   Arrange pita halves on two large cookie sheets. Bake until lightly toasted, about 3 minutes.

**5**   Spread bean mixture on toasted pitas. Top with broccoli mixture and sprinkle with soy Parmesan. Bake until heated through, 7 to 10 minutes longer. Sprinkle with tomatoes to serve.

**EACH SERVING:** ABOUT 465 CALORIES | 23G PROTEIN | 58G CARBOHYDRATE | 18G TOTAL FAT 2G SATURATED) | 13G FIBER | 0MG CHOLESTEROL | 1,195MG SODIUM

# EAT-YOUR-VEGETABLES SALADS

Salads are terrific building blocks for vegan meals. Whether you prepare a hearty main-dish salad featuring grains or pasta, or a selection of side-dish salads—such as the trio features in the photo, opposite—you can count on salads to help you create meals that are nutritious and delicious.

Although we usually think of salads as a combination of vegetables tossed with greens, this chapter encourages you to expand your definition. Pasta, grains, or beans can each serve as the foundation of a satisfying salad, as our recipes for Rice Noodles with Many Herbs, Wheat-Berry Salad with Dried Cherries, and Six-Bean Salad with Tomato Vinaigrette attest. In fact, building a salad around whole grains is a particularly smart way to create hearty main dishes. The grain serves up ample dietary fiber and protein, too. Pair it with a rainbow of fresh vegetables, greens, and/or fruit and you have a meal that's bursting with antioxidant goodness.

Although we may be most familiar with cold salads, warm salads—like our Warm Broccoli and Carrot Slaw—are worth exploring in the colder seasons. And, if you are willing to step into unfamiliar territory, we hope you will try out our recipe for Seaweed Salad. Long considered an important food source in Asian cultures, we are only just beginning to appreciate the many health benefits, and culinary applications, of this iodine-rich food.

*Clockwise from left: Barley and Corn Salad; Creamy Two-Potato Salad; Snap Pea Salad (pages 55–57)*

# LENTIL AND SPINACH SALAD

If you're concerned about eating enough protein and dietary fiber, here's a great way to get lots of both in a single salad bowl. Simmer lentils with carrots and apples, then toss with a lemon-balsamic vinaigrette and serve over dressed spinach leaves.

ACTIVE TIME: 25 MINUTES · TOTAL TIME: 40 MINUTES
MAKES: 12 SIDE-DISH SERVINGS

1½ CUPS LENTILS

2 CARROTS, PEELED AND CUT INTO ¼-INCH PIECES

2 GOLDEN DELICIOUS APPLES, CORED AND CUT INTO ¼-INCH PIECES

3 LEMONS

⅓ CUP OLIVE OIL

¼ CUP BALSAMIC VINEGAR

1½ TEASPOONS SUGAR

1½ TEASPOONS SALT

¾ TEASPOON COARSELY GROUND BLACK PEPPER

2 BAGS (10 OUNCES EACH) SPINACH, TOUGH STEMS TRIMMED (SEE TIP)

CHOPPED FRESH PARSLEY FOR GARNISH

1  Rinse lentils under cold running water and discard any stones or shriveled beans. In 4-quart saucepan, combine lentils and 8 *cups water*; heat to boiling over high heat. Stir in carrots and apples; heat to boiling. Reduce heat to low and simmer until lentils are tender, 15 to 20 minutes; drain.

2  Meanwhile, from lemons, grate 2 teaspoons peel and squeeze ¼ cup juice. In small bowl, with wire whisk or fork, mix oil, vinegar, sugar, salt, pepper, lemon juice, and lemon peel.

3  To serve, in large bowl, toss spinach with ⅓ cup dressing. Stir remaining dressing into lentil mixture. Place spinach leaves on salad plates and top with lentils. Sprinkle with parsley.

TIP To store washed greens, layer the leaves between barely dampened paper towels and place in a perforated plastic vegetable bag (sold next to the sandwich bags in the supermarket) or in a zip-tight plastic bag with a few holes poked in it. (Seal the bag loosely.) Leafy greens should stay fresh in the crisper for up to 5 days.

EACH SERVING: ABOUT 165 CALORIES | 8G PROTEIN | 20G CARBOHYDRATE | 6G TOTAL FAT (1G SATURATED) | 12G FIBER | 0MG CHOLESTEROL | 345MG SODIUM

# WARM BROCCOLI AND CARROT SLAW

Everyone—kids and adults alike—loves this healthy take on coleslaw. Add a little lemon juice to brighten the flavors.

**TOTAL TIME:** 10 MINUTES

**MAKES:** 4 SIDE-DISH SERVINGS

1 TABLESPOON VEGAN STICK MARGARINE

1 GARLIC CLOVE, CRUSHED WITH A GARLIC PRESS

2 CUPS SHREDDED BROCCOLI STEMS

2 CUPS SHREDDED CARROTS

SALT AND GROUND BLACK PEPPER

FRESH LEMON JUICE (OPTIONAL)

Melt vegan margarine in large skillet over medium-high heat. Add garlic, broccoli, and carrots. Cook 5 minutes, stirring frequently. Season with salt and pepper and, if desired, a squeeze of fresh lemon juice.

**EACH SERVING:** ABOUT 65 CALORIES | 2G PROTEIN | 9G CARBOHYDRATE | 3G TOTAL FAT (1G SATURATED) | 4G FIBER | 0MG CHOLESTEROL | 230MG SODIUM

# SIX-BEAN SALAD WITH TOMATO VINAIGRETTE

This salad is a tasty powerhouse of protein, iron, and bone-building vitamin K—in other words, it's a good choice for those who are eliminating or reducing meat from their diets. The tomato dressing contributes a zesty finish. See photo, opposite.

ACTIVE TIME: 20 MINUTES · TOTAL TIME: 26 MINUTES PLUS CHILLING
MAKES: 18 SIDE-DISH SERVINGS

1   TEASPOON SALT

8   OUNCES GREEN BEANS, TRIMMED AND CUT INTO 1-INCH PIECES

8   OUNCES WAX BEANS, TRIMMED AND CUT INTO 1-INCH PIECES

1   CAN (15 TO 19 OUNCES) GARBANZO BEANS

1   CAN (15 TO 19 OUNCES) BLACK BEANS OR BLACK SOYBEANS OR 1½ CUPS HOME-COOKED BEANS, PAGE 10

1   CAN (15 TO 19 OUNCES) RED KIDNEY BEANS OR 1½ CUPS HOME-COOKED BEANS, PAGE 10

1½ CUPS (HALF 16-OUNCE BAG) FROZEN SHELLED GREEN SOYBEANS (EDAMAME), THAWED

TOMATO VINAIGRETTE

1   SMALL RIPE TOMATO (4 OUNCES), COARSELY CHOPPED

1   SMALL SHALLOT, COARSELY CHOPPED

¼   CUP OLIVE OIL

2   TABLESPOONS RED WINE VINEGAR

1   TABLESPOON DIJON MUSTARD

½   TEASPOON SALT

¼   TEASPOON GROUND BLACK PEPPER

1   In 12-inch skillet, heat 1 inch *water* with salt to boiling over high heat. Add green and wax beans; return water to a boil. Reduce heat to low; simmer until beans are tender-crisp, 6 to 8 minutes. Drain beans. Rinse with cold running water to stop cooking; drain again. Transfer beans to large serving bowl.

2   While green and wax beans are cooking, rinse and drain garbanzo, black, and kidney beans. Add canned beans and soybeans to bowl with green and wax beans.

3   Prepare Tomato Vinaigrette: In blender, combine tomato, shallot, oil, vinegar, mustard, salt, and pepper. Blend until smooth.

4   Add vinaigrette to beans in bowl. Toss until beans are evenly coated. Cover and refrigerate at least 1 hour to blend flavors or up to 8 hours.

**EACH SERVING:** ABOUT 130 CALORIES | 7G PROTEIN | 17G CARBOHYDRATE | 4G TOTAL FAT (0G SATURATED) | 6G FIBER | 0MG CHOLESTEROL | 230MG SODIUM

# VEGAN-WISE
## ADD PROTEIN TO SALADS

When you were following a nonvegan diet, you probably simply sautéed some chicken breast, shrimp, or beef strips, and tossed them into your salad, perhaps with a little cheese. Happily, there are plenty of satisfying ways to up the protein in thoroughly vegan salads, too.

**Nuts and seeds:** Sprinkling your salads with nuts or seeds is a glorious way to add protein and heart-healthy fats, too. Don't limit yourself to walnuts and sliced almonds—consider hazelnuts, pecans, sesame seeds, or pumpkin seeds. Toasting nuts in the oven for 10 minutes or on the stovetop for 5 minutes will add flavor and fragrance to your salad du jour. See Tip, page 116.

**Beans and legumes:** Beans are a vegan's best friend. A serving of beans—canned or home-cooked—adds not only protein, but fiber and lots of vitamins, too. Black, pinto, kidney, cannellini, and garbanzo beans are obvious choices, but lentils, Great Northern beans, adzuki, edamame, and mung beans will all add color, texture—and yes—protein to greens, mixed vegetables, or pasta salads.

**Soy products:** Grilled or baked tofu slices or sautéed tempeh are great protein-rich additions to salads, especially if you marinate them in a little dressing before cooking. You can also find soy chicken and beef strips at your supermarket or health-food store—flavored or not—that will turn your garden-variety salad into a thing of beauty.

# VEGETABLES WITH SESAME VINAIGRETTE

This lively mix of green vegetables is cooked just until tender-crisp and tossed with the rich roasted flavor of sesame oil.

**ACTIVE TIME:** 25 MINUTES · **TOTAL TIME:** 30 MINUTES

**MAKES:** 10 SIDE-DISH SERVINGS

| | |
|---|---|
| 1 POUND ASPARAGUS | 2 TABLESPOONS OLIVE OR VEGETABLE OIL |
| 2 MEDIUM ZUCCHINI (8 TO 10 OUNCES EACH) | 1½ TEASPOONS SALT |
| 1 MEDIUM BUNCH BROCCOLI (16 OUNCES) | 3 TABLESPOONS SEASONED RICE VINEGAR |
| 8 OUNCES SUGAR SNAP PEAS OR SNOW PEAS | 1 TABLESPOON ASIAN SESAME OIL |
| 1 BUNCH GREEN ONIONS | ½ TEASPOON SUGAR |

1   Hold base of each asparagus stalk firmly and bend stalk; the end will break off at the spot where stalk becomes too tough to eat. Discard tough ends; trim scales if stalks are gritty. Cut asparagus into 2-inch-long pieces.

2   Cut zucchini into 1½-inch pieces. Cut broccoli into 2½-inch-long pieces. Remove stem and strings along both edges of each pea pod. Cut green onions into 1-inch pieces.

3   In 3-quart saucepan over high heat, bring 1 *inch water* to a boil over high heat. Add broccoli and bring back to boiling. Reduce heat to low; cover and simmer until broccoli is just tender-crisp, 4 to 5 minutes. Drain.

4   In nonstick 12-inch skillet, heat 1 tablespoon olive oil over medium-high heat, until hot. Add zucchini, green onions, and ¼ teaspoon salt and cook until vegetables are golden and tender-crisp, stirring frequently; with slotted spoon, remove to bowl.

5   Add remaining 1 tablespoon olive oil to oil remaining in skillet and heat until hot. Add asparagus, snap peas, and ¼ teaspoon salt and cook until vegetables are golden and tender-crisp, stirring frequently.

6   In cup, mix vinegar, sesame oil, sugar, and remaining 1 teaspoon salt. Add zucchini, green onions, and broccoli to vegetables in skillet. Stir in sesame vinaigrette, tossing to coat vegetables well; heat through. Serve vegetables warm, or cover and refrigerate to serve cold later.

**EACH SERVING:** ABOUT 85 CALORIES | 3G PROTEIN | 10G CARBOHYDRATE | 4G TOTAL FAT (0.5G SATURATED) | 3G FIBER | 0MG CHOLESTEROL | 465 MG SODIUM

# BARLEY AND CORN SALAD

This fresh summer side dish showcases vegetables that are best at their peak, including fresh corn, tomatoes, and basil. Perfect for picnics or cookouts. For photo, see page 48.

ACTIVE TIME: 15 MINUTES · TOTAL TIME: 50 MINUTES
MAKES: 12 SIDE-DISH SERVINGS

2½ CUPS WATER

1¼ CUPS PEARL BARLEY

5 MEDIUM EARS CORN, HUSKS AND SILK REMOVED

1 SMALL BUNCH BASIL

¼ CUP RICE VINEGAR

¼ CUP OLIVE OIL

1 TEASPOON SALT

¼ TEASPOON GROUND BLACK PEPPER

2 LARGE RIPE TOMATOES (10 TO 12 OUNCES EACH), CUT INTO ½-INCH CHUNKS

2 GREEN ONIONS, THINLY SLICED

1 In 2-quart saucepan, heat water to boiling over high heat. Stir in barley; heat to boiling. Reduce heat to low; cover and simmer 30 to 35 minutes or until barley is tender.

2 Meanwhile, place corn on plate in microwave oven. Cook on High 4 to 5 minutes, turning and rearranging corn halfway through cooking. Cool slightly until easy to handle. Chop enough basil leaves to equal ⅓ cup; reserve remaining basil for garnish.

3 With sharp knife, cut corn kernels from cobs. In large bowl, with fork, mix vinegar, oil, salt, and pepper; stir in corn, warm barley, tomatoes, green onions, and chopped basil until combined. If not serving right away, cover and refrigerate up to 4 hours. Garnish with basil leaves to serve.

**EACH SERVING:** ABOUT 155 CALORIES | 2G PROTEIN | 26G CARBOHYDRATE | 5G TOTAL FAT (1G SATURATED) | 5G FIBER | 0MG CHOLESTEROL | 205MG SODIUM

# SNAP PEA SALAD

This yummy double-pea salad is easy to prepare. Use any leftover fresh dill in your next soy-mayonnaise-based salad.

---

**ACTIVE TIME:** 10 MINUTES · **TOTAL TIME:** 15 MINUTES
**MAKES:** 8 SIDE-DISH SERVINGS

---

1   POUND SUGAR SNAP PEAS, STRINGS REMOVED

1   PACKAGE (10 OUNCES) FROZEN PEAS

½   CUP MINCED RED ONION

2   TABLESPOONS WHITE WINE VINEGAR

2   TABLESPOONS VEGETABLE OIL

2   TABLESPOONS CHOPPED FRESH DILL

1   TABLESPOON SUGAR

½   TEASPOON SALT

¼   TEASPOON COARSELY GROUND BLACK PEPPER

1   In 5- to 6-quart saucepot, heat *2 inches water* to boiling over high heat. Add snap peas and frozen peas; cook 1 minute. Drain vegetables; rinse under cold running water to stop cooking. Drain again; pat dry between layers of paper towels.

2   In large bowl, stir onion, vinegar, oil, dill, sugar, salt, and pepper until mixed. Add peas; toss to coat. If not serving right away, cover and refrigerate up to 4 hours.

---

**EACH SERVING:** ABOUT 100 CALORIES | 4G PROTEIN | 13G CARBOHYDRATE | 4G TOTAL FAT (0G SATURATED) | 4G FIBER | 0MG CHOLESTEROL | 245MG SODIUM

# CREAMY TWO-POTATO SALAD

This creamy, mustard-spiked potato salad is made with red and sweet potatoes. It's sure to be a new favorite on the cookout recipe roster. For photo, see page 48.

**ACTIVE TIME:** 15 MINUTES · **TOTAL TIME:** 30 MINUTES
**MAKES:** 8 SIDE-DISH SERVINGS

2   POUNDS RED POTATOES (ABOUT 8 MEDIUM), CUT INTO 1-INCH PIECES

1   POUND SWEET POTATOES (2 SMALL), CUT INTO 1-INCH PIECES

¼   CUP RED WINE VINEGAR

1   TABLESPOON SPICY BROWN MUSTARD

1¼ TEASPOONS SALT

½   TEASPOON COARSELY GROUND BLACK PEPPER

½   CUP SOY MAYONNAISE (SEE PAGE 39 TO MAKE YOUR OWN)

¼   CUP PLAIN SOY MILK

2   MEDIUM STALKS CELERY, CHOPPED

1   SMALL RED ONION, MINCED

⅓   CUP LOOSELY PACKED FRESH FLAT-LEAF PARSLEY LEAVES, CHOPPED

1   In 5- to 6-quart saucepot, place red potatoes and enough *water* to cover by 1 inch; heat to boiling over high heat. Reduce heat to low and simmer 2 minutes. Stir in sweet potatoes; heat to boiling over high heat. Reduce heat to low; cover and simmer 8 to 10 minutes or until potatoes are just fork-tender.

2   Meanwhile, in large bowl, with wire whisk, mix vinegar, mustard, salt, and pepper.

3   Drain potatoes well. While hot, add potatoes to dressing in bowl; gently stir with rubber spatula until evenly coated. Let stand until cool.

4   In small bowl, whisk soy mayonnaise and soy milk until smooth. Add mayonnaise mixture, celery, onion, and parsley to potato mixture; gently stir with rubber spatula until potatoes are well coated. Serve at room temperature, or cover and refrigerate until ready to serve.

**EACH SERVING:** ABOUT 215 CALORIES | 3G PROTEIN | 29G CARBOHYDRATE | 9G TOTAL FAT (2G SATURATED) | 4G FIBER | 0MG CHOLESTEROL | 506MG SODIUM

# RICE NOODLES WITH MANY HERBS

Whip up this light summery main-dish salad with fast-cooking rice noodles, carrots, cucumber, herbs, and our delicious Asian dressing. Serve warm or at room temperature.

---

ACTIVE TIME: 20 MINUTES · TOTAL TIME: 30 MINUTES

MAKES: 4 MAIN-DISH SERVINGS

---

3   SMALL CARROTS, PEELED AND CUT INTO 2" BY ¼" MATCHSTICK STRIPS (1⅓ CUPS)

⅓   CUP SEASONED RICE VINEGAR

1   PACKAGE (1 POUND) ½-INCH-WIDE FLAT RICE NOODLES

⅓   ENGLISH (SEEDLESS) CUCUMBER, UNPEELED AND CUT INTO 2" BY ¼" MATCHSTICK STRIPS (1 CUP)

1   CUP LOOSELY PACKED FRESH CILANTRO LEAVES

½   CUP LOOSELY PACKED FRESH MINT LEAVES

⅓   CUP LOOSELY PACKED SMALL FRESH BASIL LEAVES

⅓   CUP SNIPPED FRESH CHIVES

2   TEASPOONS ASIAN SESAME OIL

1   In small bowl, stir carrots with rice vinegar. Let stand at room temperature while preparing noodles.

2   In 8-quart saucepot, heat 5 *quarts water* to boiling over high heat. Add noodles and cook just until cooked through, about 3 minutes. Drain noodles; rinse under cold running water and drain again.

3   Transfer noodles to large shallow serving bowl. Add carrots with their liquid, cucumber, cilantro, mint, basil, chives, and sesame oil; toss well.

---

**EACH SERVING:** ABOUT 470 CALORIES | 7G PROTEIN | 105G CARBOHYDRATE | 3G TOTAL FAT (20G SATURATED) | 2G FIBER | 0MG CHOLESTEROL | 550MG SODIUM

# SHREDDED BEETS WITH CELERY AND DATES

This simple salad has high crunch appeal and showcases the rich, earthy flavor of beets.

---

TOTAL TIME: 10 MINUTES

MAKES: 8 SIDE-DISH SERVINGS

---

| | |
|---|---|
| 1 POUND BEETS, PEELED | 3 TABLESPOONS FRESH LEMON JUICE |
| 3 STALKS CELERY, THINLY SLICED | ¼ TEASPOON SALT |
| ½ CUP PITTED DRIED DATES, CHOPPED | ¼ TEASPOON COARSELY GROUND BLACK PEPPER |

**1** Cut beets into quarters. In food processor with shredding blade attached, shred beets; transfer to large bowl.

**2** Stir in celery, dates, lemon juice, salt, and pepper. If not serving right away, cover and refrigerate up to 4 hours.

---

**EACH SERVING:** ABOUT 50 CALORIES | 1G PROTEIN | 13G CARBOHYDRATE | 0G TOTAL FAT (0G SATURATED) | 2G FIBER | 0MG CHOLESTEROL | 110MG SODIUM

# COUSCOUS SALAD WITH GRAPES AND THYME

Green and red grapes, toasted pine nuts, and fresh thyme liven up couscous, a coarsely ground semolina pasta that's a staple of North African cuisine.

ACTIVE TIME: 15 MINUTES · TOTAL TIME: 20 MINUTES
MAKES: 6 SIDE-DISH SERVINGS

1   PACKAGE (10 OUNCES) WHOLE-WHEAT COUSCOUS (MOROCCAN PASTA)

1½ TEASPOONS FRESH THYME LEAVES

½   CUP CIDER VINEGAR

2   TABLESPOONS OLIVE OIL

1   TEASPOON SALT

1½ CUPS MIXED GREEN AND RED SEEDLESS GRAPES (ABOUT ½ POUND), EACH CUT INTO QUARTERS

½   CUP PINE NUTS (PIGNOLI), TOASTED

FRESH THYME SPRIGS FOR GARNISH

1   Prepare couscous as label directs, but do not use salt or margarine. Stir thyme into couscous.

2   In large bowl, mix vinegar, oil, and salt. Add grapes, pine nuts, and warm couscous; toss well to coat. Cover and refrigerate if not serving right away. Garnish with thyme sprigs to serve.

EACH SERVING: ABOUT 220 CALORIES | 6G PROTEIN | 34G CARBOHYDRATE | 7G TOTAL FAT (1G SATURATED) | 5G FIBER | 0MG CHOLESTEROL | 270MG SODIUM

# WHEAT BERRY SALAD WITH DRIED CHERRIES

This salad is a wonderful mix of textures and flavors—the chewy, nutty taste of wheat berries, combined with the pucker of tart dried cherries and lemon juice, the crunch of celery, and the hot-sweetness of Dijon and maple syrup.

**ACTIVE TIME:** 15 MINUTES · **TOTAL TIME:** 1 HOUR 30 MINUTES
**MAKES:** 12 SIDE-DISH SERVINGS

| | |
|---|---|
| 2 CUPS WHEAT BERRIES (WHOLE-WHEAT KERNELS) | 3 MEDIUM STALKS CELERY, EACH CUT LENGTHWISE IN HALF, THEN CUT CROSSWISE INTO ¼-INCH-THICK SLICES |
| 1 LARGE SHALLOT, MINCED | |
| 3 TABLESPOONS FRESH LEMON JUICE | ¾ CUP DRIED TART CHERRIES, CHOPPED |
| 1 TABLESPOON DIJON MUSTARD | ½ CUP CHOPPED FRESH FLAT-LEAF PARSLEY |
| 1 TABLESPOON OLIVE OIL | |
| 2 TEASPOONS MAPLE SYRUP | FLAT-LEAF PARSLEY SPRIGS AND LETTUCE FOR GARNISH |
| 1½ TEASPOONS SALT | |
| ½ TEASPOON COARSELY GROUND BLACK PEPPER | |

**1**  In 4-quart saucepan, heat wheat berries and *8 cups water* to boiling over high heat. Reduce heat to low; cover and simmer until wheat berries are just tender but still firm to the bite, about 1½ hours.

**2**  Meanwhile, in large bowl, with wire whisk or fork, mix shallot, lemon juice, mustard, oil, maple syrup, salt, and pepper.

**3**  When wheat berries are cooked, drain well. Add warm wheat berries to dressing with celery, cherries, and chopped parsley; toss well. Serve salad at room temperature, or cover and refrigerate until ready to serve. Garnish with parsley sprigs and lettuce.

**EACH SERVING:** ABOUT 130 CALORIES | 4G PROTEIN | 26G CARBOHYDRATE | 2G TOTAL FAT (0G SATURATED) | 6G FIBER | 0MG CHOLESTEROL | 310MG SODIUM

# NUTRIENT-RICH SEAWEED SALAD

If you've never considered eating seaweed, you should! Ounce for ounce, seaweed is higher in vitamins and minerals than any other class of food. In fact, it contains all the minerals needed for human health in proportions very similar to those found in human blood. It is particularly prized as a rich source of iodine. This recipe features dried hijiki, commonly used in Japanese home cooking and found in natural food stores or online. Soaking as directed eliminates any "fishy" taste, while the rice vinegar and sesame dressing turns this sea vegetable into a tasty salad.

**ACTIVE TIME:** 5 MINUTES · **TOTAL TIME:** 30 MINUTES
**MAKES:** 4 CUPS OR 4 SIDE-DISH SERVINGS

½ CUP DRIED HIJIKI SEAWEED

1 LARGE CARROT

3 TABLESPOONS THINLY SLICED SCALLION

3 TABLESPOONS SEASONED RICE VINEGAR

1 TEASPOON SUGAR

½ TEASPOON SESAME OIL

PINCH GROUND BLACK PEPPER

**1** Place seaweed in medium bowl and cover with 5 cups warm water. Soak 25 minutes.

**2** Meanwhile, peel and grate carrot. Place carrot and scallion in medium bowl.

**3** Drain seaweed and pat dry. Add to bowl with carrot and scallion. Mix in vinegar, sugar, sesame oil and pepper until well combined.

**EACH SERVING:** ABOUT 35 CALORIES | 0G PROTEIN | 7G CARBOHYDRATE | 0.5G TOTAL FAT (0G SATURATED) | 2G FIBER | 0MG CHOLESTEROL | 276MG SODIUM

# NOURISHING NOODLES & GRAINS

You know whole grains are good for you, but how can you incorporate them into great-tasting meals? This chapter gets you started with recipes for wholesome and delicious entrées like Garden Rice and Red Beans, Spiced Couscous with Vegetables, and, for a sweet and savory meal, Bulgur Pilaf with Garbanzo Beans and Apricots. Our Aromatic Brown Rice plus two flavorful variations allows you to prepare a fragrant bed of whole-grain goodness for your own creations—a hearty chili, tofu stir-fry, or perhaps a Moroccan stew.

And who can live without pasta? Not us! We've gathered a collection of our favorite vegan-friendly pasta dishes, ranging from tempting Soba Noodles Primavera with Miso to an easy Middle-Eastern dish composed of macaroni and spicy tomato sauce with garbanzo beans. Pasta is a great playground for vegetables: throw together our Hearty Vegetable Bolognese or Red Cabbage Spaghetti and you'll see! Pasta dinners are also another opportunity to incorporate whole grains in your family's diet. In fact, a whole-grain makeover for your favorite pasta dishes is as simple as buying whole-grain or 100-percent whole-wheat pasta instead of the egg- or semolina-based pastas you may be eating. Just be sure to read the labels closely when purchasing whole-grain pastas. For example, a pasta may proclaim itself multigrain, but if you read the label, you might find that semolina, a refined flour, is the number one ingredient.

For more ideas on how to increase your family's grain consumption, see Quick and Easy Ways to Get Your Grains (page 71).

*Bulgur Pilaf with Garbanzo Beans and Apricots (page 69)*

# AROMATIC BROWN RICE

Think of rice as a blank canvas that you can add any number of flavorings to for your own taste creation. Below is a basic recipe for cooking up brown rice, followed by three very different variations.

ACTIVE TIME: 5 MINUTES · TOTAL TIME: 50 MINUTES
MAKES: 4 SIDE-DISH SERVINGS

| | | | |
|---|---|---|---|
| 1 | CUP LONG-GRAIN BROWN RICE | ¾ | CUP WATER |
| 1 | CUP VEGETABLE BROTH | ¼ | TEASPOON SALT |

In a medium saucepan, combine rice, broth, water, and salt and bring to boiling, uncovered, over high heat. Cover and simmer over low heat until rice is tender and liquid is absorbed, 40 to 45 minutes.

EACH SERVING: ABOUT 175 CALORIES | 4G PROTEIN | 36G CARBOHYDRATE | 2G TOTAL FAT (0G SATURATED) | 3G FIBER | 0MG CHOLESTEROL | 385MG SODIUM

## ORANGE-CILANTRO BROWN RICE

After rice has cooked, stir in **2 tablespoons chopped fresh cilantro and ½ teaspoon freshly grated orange peel.**

EACH SERVING: ABOUT 175 CALORIES | 4G PROTEIN | 37G CARBOHYDRATE | 1G TOTAL FAT (0G SATURATED) | 3G FIBER | 0MG CHOLESTEROL | 295MG SODIUM

## ASIAN BROWN RICE

Omit salt when cooking rice. After rice has cooked, stir in **2 green onions,** chopped, **2 teaspoons soy sauce,** and **¼ teaspoon Asian sesame oil.**

EACH SERVING: ABOUT 180 CALORIES | 4G PROTEIN | 38G CARBOHYDRATE | 1G TOTAL FAT (0G SATURATED) | 3G FIBER | 1MG CHOLESTEROL | 380MG SODIUM

# MUSHROOM AND BARLEY PILAF

A mixture of fresh and dried mushrooms and hearty root vegetables are cooked with barley for a flavorful entrée—especially good on a crisp autumn day!

**ACTIVE TIME:** 20 MINUTES · **TOTAL TIME:** 1 HOUR 5 MINUTES

**MAKES:** 4 MAIN-DISH SERVINGS

3   CUPS BOILING WATER

1   PACKAGE (ABOUT ½ OUNCE) DRIED PORCINI MUSHROOMS (½ CUP)

2   TABLESPOONS VEGAN STICK MARGARINE OR OLIVE OIL

1   MEDIUM ONION, FINELY CHOPPED

2   MEDIUM CARROTS, PEELED, EACH CUT LENGTHWISE IN HALF, THEN CROSSWISE INTO ¼-INCH-THICK SLICES

2   MEDIUM PARSNIPS (6 OUNCES EACH), PEELED, EACH CUT LENGTHWISE IN HALF, THEN CROSSWISE INTO ¼-INCH-THICK SLICES

2   PACKAGES (4 OUNCES EACH) SLICED WILD MUSHROOM BLEND OR 8 OUNCES MIXED WILD MUSHROOMS, TOUGH STEMS DISCARDED AND CAPS THINLY SLICED

1¼ TEASPOONS SALT

¼   TEASPOON COARSELY GROUND BLACK PEPPER

¼   TEASPOON DRIED THYME

1½ CUPS PEARL BARLEY (12 OUNCES)

½   CUP LOOSELY PACKED FRESH PARSLEY LEAVES, CHOPPED

**1**   Into medium bowl, pour boiling water over dried mushrooms; let stand 10 minutes. With slotted spoon, remove porcini from soaking liquid, reserving liquid. Rinse to remove any sand; coarsely chop and set aside. Strain soaking liquid through sieve lined with paper towel into liquid measuring cup. Add enough water to liquid to equal 4½ cups total; set aside.

**2**   Meanwhile, in nonstick 5- to 6-quart Dutch oven or saucepan, melt vegan margarine over medium-high heat. Add onion, carrots, parsnips, wild mushrooms, salt, pepper, and thyme; cook until vegetables are tender-crisp, about 10 minutes, stirring occasionally.

**3**   Add barley and porcini with soaking liquid; heat to boiling. Reduce heat to medium-low; cover and simmer until barley and vegetables are tender, 35 to 40 minutes, stirring occasionally. Stir in parsley.

**EACH SERVING:** ABOUT 425 CALORIES | 12G PROTEIN | 82G CARBOHYDRATE | 7G TOTAL FAT (1G SATURATED) | 17G FIBER | 0MG CHOLESTEROL | 855MG SODIUM

# SPICED COUSCOUS WITH VEGETABLES

A blend of cumin, curry powder, and paprika enhances this tasty Moroccan-style side dish.

**ACTIVE TIME:** 15 MINUTES · **TOTAL TIME:** 30 MINUTES PLUS STANDING

**MAKES:** 4 MAIN-DISH SERVINGS

| | | | |
|---|---|---|---|
| 1 | PACKAGE (10 OUNCES) WHOLE-WHEAT COUSCOUS (MOROCCAN PASTA) | 3 | RIPE MEDIUM TOMATOES, CUT INTO ¼-INCH PIECES |
| ¼ | TEASPOON COARSELY GROUND BLACK PEPPER | 1 | TABLESPOON GROUND CUMIN |
| 2 | TABLESPOONS OLIVE OIL | 2 | TEASPOONS CURRY POWDER |
| 1 | TEASPOON SALT | 2 | TEASPOONS PAPRIKA |
| 2 | MEDIUM CARROTS, PEELED AND CUT INTO ¼-INCH PIECES | ¼ | CUP PINE NUTS (PIGNOLI), TOASTED |
| 1 | MEDIUM RED ONION, CUT INTO ¼-INCH PIECES | ¼ | CUP LOOSELY PACKED FRESH PARSLEY LEAVES, CHOPPED |
| 1 | MEDIUM ZUCCHINI, CUT INTO ¼-INCH PIECES | ¼ | CUP PITTED PRUNES, CUT INTO SLIVERS |

**1** Prepare couscous as label directs, but instead of the salt or butter called for, stir in pepper, 1 tablespoon oil, and ½ teaspoon salt; cover and keep warm.

**2** Meanwhile, in nonstick 12-inch skillet, heat remaining 1 tablespoon oil over medium heat until hot. Add carrots and onion; cook 5 minutes, stirring occasionally. Add zucchini and cook until vegetables are tender, about 5 minutes longer. Stir in tomatoes, cumin, curry, paprika, and remaining ½ teaspoon salt; cook 2 minutes longer.

**3** Stir vegetable mixture into couscous; sprinkle with pine nuts, parsley, and prunes.

**EACH SERVING:** ABOUT 460 CALORIES | 14G PROTEIN | 76G CARBOHYDRATE | 12G TOTAL FAT (2G SATURATED) | 14G FIBER | 0MG CHOLESTEROL | 570MG SODIUM

# BULGUR PILAF WITH GARBANZO BEANS AND APRICOTS

This meatless dish turns grain and beans into a hearty entrée. For photo, see page 64.

ACTIVE TIME: 10 MINUTES · TOTAL TIME: 30 MINUTES
MAKES: 4 MAIN-DISH SERVINGS

¾ CUP WATER

1 CAN (14½ OUNCES) VEGETABLE BROTH

1 CUP BULGUR

1 TABLESPOON OLIVE OIL

1 SMALL ONION, CHOPPED

2 TEASPOONS CURRY POWDER

1 GARLIC CLOVE, CRUSHED WITH GARLIC PRESS

1 CAN (15 TO 19 OUNCES) GARBANZO BEANS, RINSED AND DRAINED

½ CUP DRIED APRICOTS

½ TEASPOON SALT

¼ CUP LOOSELY PACKED FRESH PARSLEY LEAVES, CHOPPED

1 In 2-quart covered saucepan, heat water and 1¼ cups broth to boiling over high heat. Stir in bulgur; heat to boiling. Reduce heat to medium-low; cover and simmer until liquid is absorbed, 12 to 15 minutes. Remove saucepan from heat. Uncover and fluff bulgur with fork to separate grains.

2 Meanwhile, in 12-inch nonstick skillet, heat oil over medium heat 1 minute. Add onion and cook 10 minutes, stirring occasionally. Stir in curry powder and garlic; cook 1 minute. Stir in garbanzo beans, apricots, salt, and remaining broth; heat to boiling over high heat.

3 Remove skillet from heat; stir in bulgur and parsley.

EACH SERVING: ABOUT 370 CALORIES | 13G PROTEIN | 71G CARBOHYDRATE | 6G TOTAL FAT (1G SATURATED) | 15G FIBER | 0MG CHOLESTEROL | 815MG SODIUM

# GARDEN RICE AND RED BEANS

Hot pepper sauce and fire-roasted tomatoes spice up this rice and bean dish.

ACTIVE TIME: 20 MINUTES · TOTAL TIME: 55 MINUTES

MAKES: 4 MAIN-DISH SERVINGS

3 TABLESPOONS VEGETABLE OIL

2 LARGE STALKS CELERY, FINELY CHOPPED

2 LARGE CARROTS, FINELY CHOPPED

1 MEDIUM RED PEPPER (4 TO 6 OUNCES), FINELY CHOPPED

1 SMALL ONION (4 TO 6 OUNCES), FINELY CHOPPED

¼ TEASPOON EACH SALT AND GROUND BLACK PEPPER

1 CUP LONG-GRAIN WHITE RICE

3 CUPS WATER

2 GARLIC CLOVES, CRUSHED WITH GARLIC PRESS

1 TEASPOON CHILI POWDER

3 CUPS HOME-COOKED BEANS (PAGE 10) OR 2 CANS (15 OUNCES EACH) LOW-SODIUM RED KIDNEY BEANS, RINSED AND DRAINED

1 CAN (28 OUNCES) DICED FIRE-ROASTED TOMATOES

1 TABLESPOON TOMATO PASTE

1 TO 2 TEASPOONS HOT PEPPER SAUCE

½ CUP PACKED FRESH FLAT-LEAF PARSLEY, FINELY CHOPPED

1  In 4-quart saucepan, heat 2 tablespoons oil over medium-high heat until hot. Add celery, carrots, red pepper, onion, salt, and pepper; cook 5 minutes, stirring occasionally. Stir in rice until well mixed, then add water. Heat to boiling over high heat. Cover, reduce heat to medium-low, and simmer 15 minutes. Reduce heat to low and simmer 15 minutes longer.

2  Meanwhile, in 12-inch skillet, heat remaining 1 tablespoon oil over medium heat until hot. Add garlic and chili powder and cook 30 seconds or until fragrant, stirring. Stir in beans, tomatoes, and tomato paste. Reduce heat to medium-low and simmer 15 minutes, stirring occasionally. Stir in hot sauce to taste.

3  With fork, fluff rice, then stir in half of parsley; divide rice among 4 dinner plates. Top with beans and garnish with remaining parsley.

EACH SERVING: ABOUT 615 CALORIES | 20G PROTEIN | 108G CARBOHYDRATE | 12G TOTAL FAT (1.5G SATURATED) | 15G FIBER | 0MG CHOLESTEROL | 865 MG SODIUM

## QUICK AND EASY WAYS
## TO GET YOUR GRAINS

- Choose whole-wheat or whole-grain pasta instead of pasta made from refined semolina flour.

- When making a wrap or burrito, use whole-wheat or whole-kernel corn tortillas.

- Stir in cooked barley to turn your favorite canned or homemade vegetable soup into a hearty main dish.

- Slice whole-wheat or multigrain bread into ½-inch cubes; toss with olive oil and bake until golden for tasty and healthy croutons.

- Mix cooked quinoa with canned corn, soy stick margarine, and chopped basil for a new side dish.

- Sprinkle a spoonful of toasted wheat germ on your breakfast cereal (and choose a cereal that lists whole grains at the top of the ingredients list).

# RED CABBAGE SPAGHETTI WITH GOLDEN RAISINS

This savory, subtly spiced red cabbage pasta dish is rich in B vitamins and fiber—be sure to cook only until just tender to preserve its nutritional content.

ACTIVE TIME: 10 MINUTES · TOTAL TIME: 25 MINUTES
MAKES: 6 SIDE-DISH SERVINGS

2½ TEASPOONS SALT

1 SMALL HEAD RED CABBAGE (ABOUT 1½ POUNDS)

1 TABLESPOON OLIVE OIL

1 SMALL ONION, CHOPPED

1 GARLIC CLOVE, CRUSHED WITH GARLIC PRESS

1 CUP APPLE JUICE

½ CUP GOLDEN RAISINS

PINCH GROUND CLOVES

8 OUNCES THIN SPAGHETTI

1   Heat large covered saucepot of *water* and 2 teaspoons salt to boiling over high heat.

2   Meanwhile, discard any tough outer leaves from cabbage. Cut cabbage into quarters; cut core from each quarter. Thinly slice cabbage.

3   In nonstick 12-inch skillet, heat oil over medium heat. Add onion and cook about 8 minutes or until tender, stirring occasionally. Add garlic and cook 1 minute, stirring. Stir in cabbage, apple juice, raisins, cloves, and remaining ½ teaspoon salt. Cover and cook about 15 minutes or until cabbage is tender, stirring occasionally.

4   About 5 minutes before cabbage is done, add pasta to boiling water and cook as label directs.

5   Reserve ¼ *cup pasta cooking water*; drain pasta. Stir pasta into cabbage mixture in skillet; add cooking water if mixture seems dry.

**EACH SERVING:** ABOUT 255 CALORIES | 7G PROTEIN | 509G CARBOHYDRATE | 3G TOTAL FAT (0G SATURATED) | 4G FIBER | 0MG CHOLESTEROL | 275 MG SODIUM

# HEARTY VEGETABLE BOLOGNESE

This pasta and vegetable dish is made hearty with the addition of textured soy protein. High in protein and low in fat, this soy product is an inexpensive substitute for ground beef. Look for it, along with other soy products, in the refrigerator section of your produce department.

ACTIVE TIME: 20 MINUTES · TOTAL TIME: 40 MINUTES

MAKES: 4 MAIN-DISH SERVINGS

1¾ CUPS PLUS 2 TABLESPOONS WATER

1¼ CUPS TEXTURED SOY PROTEIN (THAT RESEMBLES GROUND BEEF)

2 TEASPOONS VEGETABLE OIL

2 MEDIUM CARROTS, PEELED AND THINLY SLICED

1 MEDIUM ONION, FINELY CHOPPED

1 SMALL GREEN PEPPER, FINELY CHOPPED

2 GARLIC CLOVES, CRUSHED WITH GARLIC PRESS

1 CAN (28 OUNCES) CRUSHED TOMATOES

1 TEASPOON SUGAR

2½ TEASPOONS SALT

¼ TEASPOON COARSELY GROUND BLACK PEPPER

1 PACKAGE (16 OUNCES) CORKSCREW OR ROTELLE PASTA

GRATED NONDAIRY PARMESAN SEASONING (OPTIONAL)

1   Rehydrate textured soy protein: In 2-quart saucepan, heat 1¼ cups water to boiling over high heat. Remove saucepan from heat; stir in textured soy protein and set aside.

2   In nonstick 12-inch skillet, heat oil over medium heat until hot. Add carrots, onion, green pepper, garlic, and 2 tablespoons water; cook until vegetables are tender and golden, about 15 minutes, stirring frequently.

3   Stir in rehydrated textured soy protein, tomatoes, sugar, ½ teaspoon salt, pepper, and remaining ½ cup water; heat to boiling over high heat. Reduce heat to low; cover and simmer 20 minutes.

4   Meanwhile, in large saucepot, prepare pasta as label directs, using remaining 2 teaspoons salt in water. Drain pasta; return to pot. Add sauce; toss to mix well. Serve with grated Parmesan, if you like.

EACH SERVING: ABOUT 640 CALORIES | 28G PROTEIN | 115G CARBOHYDRATE | 7G TOTAL FAT (1G SATURATED) | 13G FIBER | 0MG CHOLESTEROL | 727MG SODIUM

# SOBA NOODLES PRIMAVERA WITH MISO

This is a quick and easy Asian-inspired pasta primavera made with packaged broccoli flowerets and shredded carrots. For a nutritional boost, we used soba noodles (Japanese buckwheat noodles) and miso (concentrated soybean paste).

ACTIVE TIME: 20 MINUTES · TOTAL TIME: 40 MINUTES

MAKES: 4 MAIN-DISH SERVINGS

1 PACKAGE (16 OUNCES) EXTRA-FIRM TOFU, DRAINED AND PATTED DRY

1 PACKAGE (8 OUNCES) SOBA NOODLES

1 TABLESPOON OLIVE OIL

1 MEDIUM RED PEPPER (4 TO 6 OUNCES), THINLY SLICED

1 LARGE ONION (12 OUNCES), SLICED

2 GARLIC CLOVES, CRUSHED WITH GARLIC PRESS

1 TABLESPOON GRATED, PEELED FRESH GINGER

¼ TEASPOON CRUSHED RED PEPPER

1 BAG (16 OUNCES) BROCCOLI FLOWERETS, CUT INTO 1½-INCH PIECES

1 BAG (10 OUNCES) SHREDDED CARROTS

¼ CUP WATER

¼ CUP RED (DARK) MISO PASTE

2 GREEN ONIONS, THINLY SLICED

1 Cut tofu horizontally in half. Cut each half into 1-inch pieces; set aside.

2 In large saucepot, prepare noodles as label directs.

3 Meanwhile, in nonstick 5- to 6-quart Dutch oven, heat oil over medium-high heat until hot. Add red pepper and onion; cook until golden, about 10 minutes, stirring occasionally. Add garlic, ginger, crushed red pepper, and tofu; cook 1 minute, stirring. Add broccoli, carrots, and water; heat to boiling over medium-high heat. Reduce heat to medium; cover and cook until vegetables are tender, about 7 minutes.

4 When noodles have cooked to desired doneness, drain, reserving ¾ cup cooking water. Return noodles to saucepot.

5 With wire whisk, mix miso paste into reserved noodle cooking water until blended.

6 To serve, toss noodles with tofu mixture, green onions, and miso-paste mixture.

EACH SERVING: ABOUT 455 CALORIES | 26G PROTEIN | 68G CARBOHYDRATE | 11G TOTAL FAT (2G SATURATED) | 11G FIBER | 0MG CHOLESTEROL | 1,290MG SODIUM

# MIDDLE-EASTERN GARBANZO BEANS AND MACARONI

A flavorful entrée based on pantry staples—canned garbanzo beans and crushed tomatoes—tossed with pasta.

ACTIVE TIME: 10 MINUTES · TOTAL TIME: 35 MINUTES

MAKES: 6 MAIN-DISH SERVINGS

12 OUNCES MACARONI TWISTS OR ELBOW MACARONI

1 TABLESPOON OLIVE OIL

1 TABLESPOON VEGAN STICK MARGARINE

1 LARGE ONION (12 OUNCES), CUT INTO ¼-INCH PIECES

2 GARLIC CLOVES, CRUSHED WITH GARLIC PRESS

1 TEASPOON SALT

1 TEASPOON GROUND CUMIN

¾ TEASPOON GROUND CORIANDER

¼ TEASPOON GROUND ALLSPICE

¼ TEASPOON COARSELY GROUND BLACK PEPPER

1 CAN (28 OUNCES) CRUSHED TOMATOES

1 CAN (15 TO 19 OUNCES) GARBANZO BEANS, RINSED AND DRAINED

¼ CUP LOOSELY PACKED FRESH PARSLEY LEAVES, CHOPPED

PARSLEY SPRIGS FOR GARNISH

1  In large saucepot, cook pasta as label directs.

2  Meanwhile, in nonstick 12-inch skillet, heat oil with margarine over medium heat until hot and melted. Add onion and cook, stirring occasionally, until tender and golden, about 20 minutes. Stir in garlic, salt, cumin, coriander, allspice, and pepper; cook 1 minute.

3  Add tomatoes and garbanzo beans to skillet; heat to boiling over medium-high heat. Reduce heat to medium low; simmer, stirring occasionally, 5 minutes.

4  Drain pasta; return to saucepot. Toss garbanzo-bean mixture with pasta; heat through. Toss with chopped parsley just before serving. Garnish with parsley sprigs.

**EACH SERVING:** ABOUT 400 CALORIES | 14G PROTEIN | 73G CARBOHYDRATE | 7G TOTAL FAT (2G SATURATED) | 5G FIBER | 5MG CHOLESTEROL | 1,039MG SODIUM

# POLENTA WITH SPICY EGGPLANT SAUCE

A great dinner you can whip up after you get home from work: Polenta cooks in the microwave oven with minimal attention while you prepare a quick skillet sauce. See photo, opposite.

ACTIVE TIME: 15 MINUTES · TOTAL TIME: 40 MINUTES
MAKES: 4 MAIN-DISH SERVINGS

1   TABLESPOON OLIVE OIL

1   MEDIUM ONION, FINELY CHOPPED

2   SMALL EGGPLANTS (ABOUT 1 POUND EACH), CUT INTO 1-INCH CHUNKS

1   GARLIC CLOVE, CRUSHED WITH GARLIC PRESS

¼   TEASPOON CRUSHED RED PEPPER

1   CAN (28 OUNCES) CRUSHED TOMATOES

1½ TEASPOONS SALT

2   CUPS PLAIN SOY MILK

1½ CUPS YELLOW CORNMEAL

GRATED NONDAIRY PARMESAN SEASONING (OPTIONAL)

PARSLEY SPRIGS (OPTIONAL)

1   In nonstick 12-inch skillet, heat oil over medium heat. Add onion and cook 5 minutes, stirring occasionally. Increase heat to medium-high; add eggplant and cook 8 minutes or until golden and tender, stirring occasionally. Add garlic and crushed red pepper, and cook 1 minute, stirring. Add tomatoes, ½ teaspoon salt, and ½ *cup water*; heat to boiling. Reduce heat to low; cover and simmer 10 minutes, stirring occasionally.

2   Meanwhile, in deep 4-quart microwave-safe bowl or casserole, combine milk, cornmeal, 1 teaspoon salt, and 4½ *cups water*. Cook in microwave oven on High 15 to 20 minutes, until thickened. After first 5 minutes of cooking, whisk vigorously until smooth (mixture will be lumpy at first), and 2 more times during remaining cooking time.

3   To serve, spoon polenta into 4 bowls; top with eggplant sauce. Garnish each serving with some grated Parmesan and a parsley sprig, if you like.

EACH SERVING: ABOUT 380 CALORIES | 13G PROTEIN | 71G CARBOHYDRATE | 6G TOTAL FAT (2G SATURATED) | 12G FIBER | 0MG CHOLESTEROL | 1,235MG SODIUM

# SOMETHING NEW...
# MAKE POLENTA LIKE A PRO

Long a staple in northern Italy, the popularity of this healthful and versatile dish has spread. On page 78, we provide quick and easy microwave directions, but if you want to know how to make a creamy polenta the old-school way, read on. Get ready to stir!

---

ACTIVE TIME: 5 MINUTES · TOTAL TIME: 35 MINUTES
MAKES: 8 SIDE-DISH SERVINGS

---

2   CUPS COLD WATER

1   TEASPOON SALT

1½  CUPS YELLOW CORNMEAL

4½  CUPS BOILING WATER

4   TABLESPOONS VEGAN STICK MARGARINE, CUT INTO PIECES

½   CUP GRATED NONDAIRY PARMESAN SEASONING (OPTIONAL)

**1**  In 5-quart Dutch oven, combine cold water and salt. With wire whisk, gradually beat in cornmeal until smooth. Whisk in boiling water. Heat to boiling over high heat. Reduce heat to medium-low and cook until mixture is very thick, 20 to 25 minutes, stirring frequently with wooden spoon.
**2**  Stir margarine and grated Parmesan, if using, into polenta until margarine has melted. Serve immediately.

---

**EACH SERVING:** ABOUT 175 CALORIES | 5G PROTEIN | 20G CARBOHYDRATE | 8G TOTAL FAT (5G SATURATED) | 1G FIBER | 20 MG CHOLESTEROL | 464MG SODIUM

# GREAT GRILLING

Just because you've gone meatless doesn't mean you've got to give away the grill. Vegetables become absolutely irresistible when they've been flame-roasted—the fire concentrates their sugars and adds that great charry flavor we all love so much. See our Guide to Grilled Vegetables, page 83, for the basics to get you started.

You'll find a range of great grilled food here, from Grilled Vegetables with Thai Pesto and other substantial salads to melty Grilled Corn and Jack Quesadillas. Serve these as party starters or the main dish with additional sides. We've also included recipes for tempeh and tofu kabobs—because who doesn't enjoy succulent tidbits served on a stick? Our Guide to Soy Meat Alternatives (page 93) will help you navigate the grocery store aisles, so you can bring home satisfying options to marinate then toss onto the grill.

Meatless doesn't mean burgerless; we've included a recipe for Southwestern Black Bean Burgers that makes a great entrée for any cookout. And our toothsome Portobello Burgers are sure to please vegans and carnivores alike. Try serving them on sourdough toast.

*Grilled Eggplant Caponata Salad (page 82)*

# GRILLED EGGPLANT CAPONATA SALAD

Grilling eggplant adds a luscious smokiness. This delicious salad of fresh tomatoes, sweet raisins, briny capers, and olives combined with grilled onions, celery, and eggplant will be a recipe you go back to again and again. For photo, see page 80.

**ACTIVE TIME:** 25 MINUTES · **TOTAL TIME:** 35 MINUTES PLUS STANDING

**MAKES:** 16 SIDE-DISH SERVINGS

| | | | |
|---|---|---|---|
| 2 | SMALL RED ONIONS, CUT INTO ½-INCH-THICK SLICES | ¼ | TEASPOON COARSELY GROUND BLACK PEPPER |
| 2 | SMALL EGGPLANTS (1 TO 1¼ POUNDS EACH), CUT INTO ¾-INCH-THICK SLICES | 6 | RIPE MEDIUM PLUM TOMATOES (1½ POUNDS), CUT INTO ½-INCH PIECES |
| | NONSTICK COOKING SPRAY | 1 | CUP KALAMATA, GAETA, OR GREEN SICILIAN OLIVES, PITTED AND CHOPPED |
| 4 | MEDIUM STALKS CELERY | ¼ | CUP GOLDEN RAISINS |
| ½ | TEASPOON SALT | 3 | TABLESPOONS DRAINED CAPERS |
| 2 | TABLESPOONS RED WINE VINEGAR | ½ | CUP LOOSELY PACKED FRESH FLAT-LEAF PARSLEY LEAVES |
| 2 | TABLESPOONS EXTRA-VIRGIN OLIVE OIL | | |
| 1 | TEASPOON SUGAR | | |

1  Prepare outdoor grill for covered direct grilling over medium heat.

2  Meanwhile, for easier handling, insert metal skewers through onion slices, if you like. Lightly spray both sides of eggplant slices with cooking spray. Sprinkle onions, eggplants, and celery with salt.

3  Place onions, eggplants, and celery on hot grill rack over medium heat. Cover grill and grill vegetables until tender and lightly browned, 8 to 10 minutes, turning once and transferring to plate as they are done. Cool slightly until easy to handle.

4  Cut eggplants and celery into ¾-inch pieces; coarsely chop onions. In large bowl, mix vinegar, oil, sugar, and pepper until blended. Stir in tomatoes, olives, raisins, capers, and parsley. Add eggplant, onions, and celery; gently toss to coat.

5  Serve salad at room temperature, or if not serving immediately, cover and refrigerate up to 1 day.

**EACH SERVING:** ABOUT 75 CALORIES | 1G PROTEIN | 11G CARBOHYDRATE | 3G TOTAL FAT (1G SATURATED) | 2G FIBER | 0MG CHOLESTEROL | 240MG SODIUM

# VEGAN-WISE
## A GUIDE TO GRILLED VEGETABLES

Vegans can eat their fill at the barbecue, too. Preheat the grill to medium-high. **MAKES:** 4 SERVINGS

| VEGETABLE | PREPARATION | SEASONING | GRILLING TIME |
|---|---|---|---|
| 8 ears corn | Soak 15 minutes, then remove silk (leave husks on) or remove husks and silk. | Brush with 1 tablespoon oil. | 45 minutes. 20 minutes, turning occasionally. |
| 1½-pound eggplant | Cut crosswise into ½-inch-thick slices. | Brush with 4 teaspoons oil. | 11 to 13 minutes per side. |
| 4 yellow squash or zucchini (8 ounces each) | Cut lengthwise into ¼-inch-thick slices. | Brush with 4 teaspoons oil. | 5 minutes per side. |
| 8 ounces large white mushrooms | Trim and thread onto skewers. | Brush with 2 teaspoons oil. | 20 minutes, turning several times. |
| 4 large portobello mushrooms (about 1 pound) | Remove stems. | Brush with 4 teaspoons oil. | 15 minutes per side. |
| 4 bell peppers | Cut lengthwise into quarters. | | 10 to 12 minutes per side. |
| 4 medium red or white onions | Cut crosswise into ½-inch-thick slices; secure with toothpicks. | Brush with 4 teaspoons oil. | 12 to 14 minutes per side. |

# GRILLED VEGETABLES WITH THAI PESTO

Pesto takes a Thai-inspired twist when we add fresh lime juice and sweet chili sauce to the mix.

**TOTAL TIME:** 25 MINUTES

**MAKES:** 4 MAIN-DISH SERVINGS

### THAI PESTO

1 LARGE LIME

½ CUP WALNUTS

1 CUP PACKED FRESH BASIL LEAVES

1 TABLESPOON THAI SWEET CHILI SAUCE

3 TABLESPOONS WATER

¼ TEASPOON SALT

### GRILLED VEGETABLES

4 PLUM TOMATOES, CUT LENGTHWISE IN HALF

2 MEDIUM YELLOW PEPPERS, CUT INTO QUARTERS AND SEEDED

½ MEDIUM EGGPLANT, CUT CROSSWISE INTO ¾-INCH-THICK SLICES

1 LARGE ZUCCHINI (10 OUNCES), CUT DIAGONALLY INTO ½-INCH-THICK SLICES

½ LARGE SWEET ONION, CUT LENGTHWISE INTO 6 WEDGES

OLIVE OIL NONSTICK COOKING SPRAY

¼ TEASPOON SALT

**1** Prepare Thai Pesto: From lime, grate ½ teaspoon peel and squeeze 2 tablespoons juice. In skillet, toast walnuts over medium heat 5 minutes, stirring until fragrant. Set aside.

**2** In food processor with knife blade attached, blend nuts, basil, chili sauce, water, lime peel and juice, and salt. Store covered in refrigerator up to 2 days. Makes about ⅔ cup.

**3** Prepare Grilled Vegetables: Prepare outdoor grill for covered direct grilling over medium heat, or heat large ridged grill pan over medium heat until hot. Lightly spray vegetables with cooking spray. Place vegetables on grill. Cover and grill tomatoes and zucchini 6 to 8 minutes, peppers and onion 8 to 10 minutes, and eggplant 10 to 12 minutes or until vegetables are tender, turning over once. Transfer vegetables to serving plate as they are done; sprinkle with salt. Serve with Thai Pesto.

**EACH SERVING:** ABOUT 205 CALORIES | 6G PROTEIN | 28G CARBOHYDRATE | 7G TOTAL FAT (1G SATURATED) | 3G FIBER | 0MG CHOLESTEROL | 365MG SODIUM

# HOISIN-GINGER TOFU AND VEGGIES

A great hoisin-ginger glaze flavors tofu, zucchini, and red pepper. Be sure to buy extra-firm tofu; other varieties will fall apart while grilling.

TOTAL TIME: 30 MINUTES

MAKES: 4 MAIN-DISH SERVINGS

### HOISIN-GINGER GLAZE

½  CUP HOISIN SAUCE

2  GARLIC CLOVES, CRUSHED WITH GARLIC PRESS

1  TABLESPOON VEGETABLE OIL

1  TABLESPOON REDUCED-SODIUM SOY SAUCE

1  TABLESPOON GRATED, PEELED FRESH GINGER

1  TABLESPOON SEASONED RICE VINEGAR

⅛  TEASPOON GROUND RED PEPPER (CAYENNE)

### TOFU AND VEGGIES

1  PACKAGE (16 OUNCES) EXTRA-FIRM TOFU, DRAINED

2  MEDIUM ZUCCHINI (8 TO 10 OUNCES EACH), EACH CUT LENGTHWISE INTO QUARTERS, THEN CROSSWISE IN HALF

1  LARGE RED PEPPER (8 TO 10 OUNCES), CUT INTO QUARTERS

1  BUNCH GREEN ONIONS

1  TEASPOON VEGETABLE OIL

1   Prepare outdoor grill for direct grilling over medium heat.

2   Prepare Hoisin-Ginger Glaze: In small bowl, with fork, mix hoisin sauce, garlic, oil, soy sauce, ginger, vinegar, and ground red pepper until blended.

3   Prepare Tofu and Veggies: Cut tofu horizontally into 4 pieces, then cut each piece crosswise in half. Place tofu on paper towels; pat dry with additional paper towels. Arrange tofu on large plate and brush both sides of tofu with half of glaze. Spoon remaining half of glaze into medium bowl; add zucchini and red pepper. Gently toss vegetables to coat with glaze. On another plate, rub green onions with oil.

4   Place tofu, zucchini, and red pepper on hot grill rack over medium heat. Grill tofu about 6 minutes, gently turning once with wide metal spatula. Transfer tofu to platter; keep warm. Continue cooking vegetables, transferring them to platter with tofu as they are done, until tender and browned, about 5 minutes longer. Add green onions to grill rack during last minute of cooking time; transfer to platter when tender.

EACH SERVING: ABOUT 245 CALORIES | 15G PROTEIN | 22G CARBOHYDRATE | 11G TOTAL FAT (1G SATURATED) | 5G FIBER | 0MG CHOLESTEROL | 615MG SODIUM

# PORTOBELLO BURGERS

We marinate these "burgers" in a broth mixture accented with thyme before grilling them, and serve on toast with a lemon and green-onion mayonnaise.

**ACTIVE TIME:** 10 MINUTES · **TOTAL TIME:** 30 MINUTES PLUS STANDING

**MAKES:** 4 SANDWICHES

¼ CUP VEGETABLE BROTH

2 TABLESPOONS OLIVE OIL

2 TEASPOONS BALSAMIC VINEGAR

1 TEASPOON FRESH THYME LEAVES

¼ TEASPOON SALT

¼ TEASPOON COARSELY GROUND BLACK PEPPER

4 MEDIUM (ABOUT 4-INCH) PORTOBELLO MUSHROOMS, STEMS DISCARDED

1 LEMON

⅓ CUP SOY MAYONNAISE (SEE PAGE 39 TO MAKE YOUR OWN)

1 SMALL GREEN ONION, MINCED

8 SLICES SOURDOUGH TOAST

1 BUNCH ARUGULA, TRIMMED

**1** In glass baking dish, just large enough to hold mushrooms in single layer, mix broth, oil, vinegar, thyme, ⅛ teaspoon salt, and ⅛ teaspoon pepper. Add mushrooms, turning to coat. Let stand 30 minutes, turning occasionally.

**2** Meanwhile, from lemon, grate ½ teaspoon peel and squeeze ½ teaspoon juice. In small bowl, stir lemon peel, lemon juice, soy mayonnaise, green onion, remaining ⅛ teaspoon salt, and remaining ⅛ teaspoon pepper.

**3** Prepare outdoor grill or heat ridged grill pan over medium heat until hot. Add mushrooms and grill, turning occasionally and brushing with remaining marinade, until mushrooms are browned and cooked through, 8 to 10 minutes per side.

**4** Spread four slices of toast with mayonnaise mixture; top with arugula and warm mushrooms. Cover with remaining toast.

**EACH SERVING:** ABOUT 320 CALORIES | 8G PROTEIN | 29G CARBOHYDRATE | 20G TOTAL FAT (4G SATURATED) | 3G FIBER | 0MG CHOLESTEROL | 518MG SODIUM

# SOUTHWESTERN BLACK BEAN BURGERS

These zesty burgers will be appreciated by everyone at the barbecue.

---

**ACTIVE TIME:** 15 MINUTES · **TOTAL TIME:** 20 MINUTES

**MAKES:** 4 BURGERS

---

1 CAN (15 TO 19 OUNCES) BLACK BEANS, RINSED AND DRAINED, OR 1½ CUPS HOME-COOKED BEANS, PAGE 10

2 TABLESPOONS SOY MAYONNAISE (SEE PAGE 39 TO MAKE YOUR OWN)

¼ CUP LOOSELY PACKED FRESH CILANTRO LEAVES, CHOPPED

1 TABLESPOON PLAIN DRIED BREAD CRUMBS

½ TEASPOON GROUND CUMIN

½ TEASPOON HOT PEPPER SAUCE

NONSTICK COOKING SPRAY

1 CUP LOOSELY PACKED SLICED LETTUCE

4 MINI (4-INCH) WHOLE-WHEAT PITA BREADS, WARMED

½ CUP MILD SALSA

**1** Prepare outdoor grill for direct grilling over medium heat.

**2** In large bowl, with potato masher or fork, mash black beans with soy mayonnaise until almost smooth (some lumps of beans should remain). Stir in cilantro, bread crumbs, cumin, and hot pepper sauce until combined. With lightly floured hands, shape bean mixture into four 3-inch round patties. Spray both sides of each patty lightly with cooking spray.

**3** Place burgers on hot grill rack over medium heat. Grill burgers until lightly browned, about 6 minutes, turning once.

**4** Arrange lettuce on pitas; top with burgers and salsa.

---

**EACH SERVING:** ABOUT 265 CALORIES | 11G PROTEIN | 42G CARBOHYDRATE | 6G TOTAL FAT (1G SATURATED) | 11G FIBER | 5MG CHOLESTEROL | 750MG SODIUM

# GRILLED VEGETABLE BURRITOS

Serve with your favorite salsa and a dollop of nondairy sour cream. The burritos may be cut into bite-size portions to create appetizers.

**ACTIVE TIME:** 25 MINUTES · **TOTAL TIME:** 40 MINUTES

**MAKES:** 4 MAIN-DISH SERVINGS

1 TABLESPOON PLUS 1 TEASPOON VEGETABLE OIL

1 TEASPOON CHILI POWDER

1 TEASPOON GROUND CUMIN

½ TEASPOON SALT

¼ TEASPOON COARSELY GROUND BLACK PEPPER

2 MEDIUM ZUCCHINI (8 TO 10 OUNCES EACH), CUT LENGTHWISE INTO ¼-INCH-THICK SLICES

1 LARGE ONION (12 OUNCES), CUT INTO ½-INCH-THICK SLICES

1 MEDIUM RED PEPPER (4 TO 6 OUNCES), CUT INTO QUARTERS

1 MEDIUM GREEN PEPPER (4 TO 6 OUNCES), CUT INTO QUARTERS

4 BURRITO-SIZED (10-INCH) FLOUR TORTILLAS

NONDAIRY SOUR CREAM

½ CUP LOOSELY PACKED FRESH CILANTRO LEAVES

BOTTLED SALSA (OPTIONAL)

**1** Prepare outdoor grill for direct grilling over medium heat.

**2** In small bowl, mix oil, chili powder, cumin, salt, and black pepper. Brush one side of zucchini slices, onion slices, and red and green pepper pieces with oil mixture.

**3** Place vegetables, oiled side down, on hot grill rack over medium heat; grill until tender and golden, 15 to 20 minutes, turning once and transferring vegetables to plate as they are done.

**4** Arrange one-fourth of grilled vegetables down center of each tortilla and dollop with nondairy sour cream. Sprinkle with cilantro, then fold sides of tortillas over filling. Serve with salsa, if you like.

**EACH SERVING:** ABOUT 330 CALORIES | 11G PROTEIN | 43G CARBOHYDRATE | 11G TOTAL FAT (2G SATURATED) | 7G FIBER | 5MG CHOLESTEROL | 655MG SODIUM

# GRILLED CORN AND JACK QUESADILLAS

These quesadillas make a fun and simple summertime meal. To save time, grate the cheese for the quesadillas while the corn is grilling. You may notice that soy cheese doesn't get as melty as dairy cheese; in this cases, that's not a bad thing, as you'll avoid having to clean strings of cheese off the grill when the meal is done!

ACTIVE TIME: 15 MINUTES · TOTAL TIME: 20 MINUTES PLUS COOLING

MAKES: 4 MAIN-DISH SERVINGS

3   LARGE EARS CORN, HUSKS AND SILK REMOVED

4   LOW-FAT BURRITO-SIZE (8- TO 10-INCH) FLOUR TORTILLAS

4   OUNCES SOY MONTEREY JACK CHEESE, SHREDDED (1 CUP)

½   CUP MILD OR MEDIUM-HOT SALSA

2   GREEN ONIONS, THINLY SLICED

1   Prepare outdoor grill for covered direct grilling over medium-high heat.

2   Place corn on hot grill rack over medium-high heat. Cover grill and cook corn, turning frequently, until brown in spots, 10 to 15 minutes.

3   Transfer corn to plate; set aside until cool enough to handle. When cool, with sharp knife, cut kernels from cobs.

4   Place tortillas on work surface. Evenly divide soy Monterey Jack, salsa, green onions, and corn on half of each tortilla. Fold tortilla over filling to make 4 quesadillas.

5   Place quesadillas on hot grill rack. Grill quesadillas, turning once, until browned on both sides, 1 to 2 minutes. Transfer to cutting board; cut each quesadilla into 3 pieces.

EACH SERVING: ABOUT 305 CALORIES | 9G PROTEIN | 50G CARBOHYDRATE | 10G TOTAL FAT (1G SATURATED) | 7G FIBER | 0MG CHOLESTEROL | 689MG SODIUM

# BBQ TEMPEH AND VEGETABLE KABOBS

These hearty barbecued tempeh and vegetable kabobs are full of classic barbecue flavor. If you are not familiar with tempeh, see our Guide to Soy Meat Alternatives, opposite, for details.

**ACTIVE TIME:** 30 MINUTES · **TOTAL TIME:** 40 MINUTES

**MAKES:** 12 SKEWERS OR 6 SERVINGS

1   PACKAGE (8 OUNCES) TEMPEH

⅔   CUP BARBECUE SAUCE

1   MEDIUM RED PEPPER, SEEDED AND CUT INTO 1-INCH PIECES

1   SMALL RED ONION, CUT INTO 6 WEDGES, EACH WEDGE HALVED

1   MEDIUM ZUCCHINI, CUT INTO ¼-INCH-THICK HALF MOONS

1   TABLESPOON CANOLA OIL PLUS ADDITIONAL FOR GRILL

SALT AND GROUND BLACK PEPPER

1   TEASPOON CHILI POWDER

12   WOODEN SKEWERS

**1**   Prepare outdoor grill for direct grilling over medium heat.

**2**   Cut tempeh into 24 cubes, about 1-inch each.

**3**   Heat nonstick 10-inch skillet over medium heat. Add tempeh and barbecue sauce and simmer until sauce thickens and sticks to tempeh, about 15 minutes, stirring occasionally. Remove from heat.

**4**   Meanwhile, cut red pepper into 1-inch pieces. Cut onion into 6 wedges, then cut each in half crosswise. Cut zucchini in half lengthwise, then crosswise into ¼-inch slices. In medium bowl, toss vegetables with 1 tablespoon oil, salt and pepper to taste, and chili powder.

**5**   Assemble skewers using everything twice, except the onion (use that only once).

**6**   Place kabobs on grill. Grill, turning occasionally until browned and tender, 12 to 15 minutes. Remove to large platter.

**EACH SERVING:** ABOUT 160 CALORIES | 9G PROTEIN | 208G CARBOHYDRATE | 6G TOTAL FAT (1G SATURATED) | 4G FIBER | 0MG CHOLESTEROL | 354 MG SODIUM

# VEGAN-WISE
# A GUIDE TO SOY MEAT ALTERNATIVES

If you're new to la vida vegan, the soy products in the grocery store refrigerator case can be mystifying. Here's an explanation of the most common ones found in large supermarkets, health-food stores, and specialty markets, plus tips on storage.

**Tofu:** This is soybean curd that is drained and pressed in a process similar to cheese-making. The creamiest tofu (with the least liquid pressed out) is soft or silken. (Use it in shakes, dressings, and dips.) Extracting still more liquid produces regular tofu, then firm, and finally extra-firm (excellent grilled or in stir-fries). Look for nonfat, low-fat, and full-fat varieties. Avoid bulk tofu, unpackaged blocks sold in water; it can be contaminated with bacteria. Sealed water-packed tofu and the aseptically packaged kind (unrefrigerated) are much safer. To store tofu after opening, cover with cool water and refrigerate for up to 1 week; change water daily.

**Tempeh (TEHM-pay):** A dense, chewy cake, this meat alternative is made from cooked, fermented soybeans. Like other soy products, tempeh absorbs the flavor of the ingredients it's cooked with, even though it has a smoky flavor of its own. Tempeh is sold refrigerated or frozen; try in soups or stir-fries or on the grill, as kabobs.

**Textured Vegetable Protein (TVP):** Also known as textured soy protein, these dried granules made from defatted soy flakes have to be rehydrated in water before cooking. TVP is a great substitute in any recipe that traditionally calls for ground beef, like our South-of-the-Border Burrito Wraps (page 117). Commercially, TVP is used to make soy hot dogs and veggie burgers.

# GLOBE-TROTTING DISHES

To keep things interesting, we've raided our archives for a selection of recipes that will satiate your desire for great flavor and give you a glimpse of vegetable-based cooking from other countries.

Beans and other legumes are an important part of the vegan diet, and the soup pot is where they really shine. Because they are the most significant source of plant-based protein, and supply a host of other important nutrients, too, if you're a vegan (or responsible for feeding one), it's worth your while to get cozy with soups and stews. A big pot of Red Lentil and Vegetable Soup or Gingery Chickpea and Tomato Stew will always provide a warm welcome to friends and family.

Soups and stews are also a great vehicle for grains. Consider our wholesome Mushroom and Brown Rice Soup, or add cooked grains to your own creations. Any kind of cooked grain will be a healthful and tasty addition to soup, so think global—barley, wild rice, hominy, wheat berries, or soba noodles are all worth your consideration.

And, don't forget the tofu. A wonderful source of protein and iron, tofu is also a flavor sponge. It soaks up the sauce in stir-fries—check out Tofu in a Spicy Brown Sauce—and would also be a delicious addition to any Asian-style broth.

*Not Your Grandma's Borscht (page 102)*

# MUSHROOM AND BROWN RICE SOUP

**Instead of the more traditional barley, we prepare our version of this hearty soup with instant brown rice, which reduces the cooking time.**

**ACTIVE TIME:** 25 MINUTES · **TOTAL TIME:** 30 MINUTES
**MAKES:** 8 CUPS OR 4 MAIN-DISH SERVINGS

| | | | |
|---|---|---|---|
| 1 | TABLESPOON OLIVE OIL | ¼ | TEASPOON DRIED THYME |
| 1 | MEDIUM ONION, FINELY CHOPPED | ⅛ | TEASPOON GROUND BLACK PEPPER |
| 1 | PACKAGE (10 OUNCES) ASSORTED SLICED WILD MUSHROOMS | 1 | CONTAINER (32 OUNCES) VEGETABLE BROTH |
| 1 | CUP BAGGED SHREDDED CARROTS | ¾ | CUP INSTANT (10-MINUTE) BROWN RICE |
| 1 | GARLIC CLOVE, CRUSHED WITH GARLIC PRESS | 2 | CUPS WATER |
| ½ | TEASPOON SALT | | |

**1** In 4-quart saucepan, heat oil over medium-high heat until hot. Add onion and cook 5 minutes, stirring occasionally. Add mushrooms and carrots and cook, stirring occasionally, until golden and tender, 8 to 10 minutes. Add garlic, salt, thyme, and pepper; cook 1 minute, stirring.

**2** Add broth, rice, and water; cover and heat to boiling over high heat. Reduce heat to medium; cook, partially covered, until rice is tender, about 5 minutes.

**EACH SERVING:** ABOUT 170 CALORIES | 8G PROTEIN | 24G CARBOHYDRATE | 6G TOTAL FAT (1G SATURATED) | 4G FIBER | 0MG CHOLESTEROL | 1,260MG SODIUM

# GAZPACHO WITH CILANTRO CREAM

Recipes for gazpacho abound. This version is topped with a dollop of cilantro-spiked nondairy sour cream, a tasty combination. For photo, see page 15.

**TOTAL TIME:** 30 MINUTES PLUS CHILLING

**MAKES:** 4 CUPS OR 4 FIRST-COURSE SERVINGS

2   MEDIUM CUCUMBERS (8 OUNCES EACH), PEELED

1   MEDIUM YELLOW PEPPER (4 TO 6 OUNCES)

¼   SMALL RED ONION

2   POUNDS RIPE TOMATOES (5 MEDIUM), PEELED, SEEDED, AND CHOPPED

½   TO 1 SMALL JALAPEÑO CHILE, SEEDED

3   TABLESPOONS FRESH LIME JUICE

2   TABLESPOONS EXTRA-VIRGIN OLIVE OIL

¾   TEASPOON PLUS ⅛ TEASPOON SALT

¼   CUP NONDAIRY SOUR CREAM OR NONDAIRY PLAIN YOGURT

1   TABLESPOON PLAIN SOY MILK

4   TEASPOONS CHOPPED FRESH CILANTRO

**1**   Coarsely chop half of 1 cucumber, half the yellow pepper, and all the onion; set aside. Cut remaining cucumbers and yellow pepper into large pieces for pureeing.

**2**   In blender or food processor with knife blade attached, puree large pieces of cucumber and yellow pepper, tomatoes, jalapeño, lime juice, oil, and ¾ teaspoon salt until smooth. Pour puree into bowl; add coarsely chopped cucumber, yellow pepper, and onion. Cover and refrigerate until well chilled, at least 6 hours and up to overnight.

**3**   Prepare cilantro cream: In small bowl, stir nondairy sour cream, soy milk, cilantro, and remaining ⅛ teaspoon salt until smooth. Cover and refrigerate.

**4**   To serve, top soup with dollops of cilantro cream.

**EACH SERVING:** ABOUT 145 CALORIES | 3G PROTEIN | 15G CARBOHYDRATE | 9G TOTAL FAT (1G SATURATED) | 4G FIBER | 0MG CHOLESTEROL | 539MG SODIUM

# JALAPEÑO-SPIKED BLACK BEAN SOUP

This flavorful Tex-Mex soup uses the hand blender to make quick work of turning a chunky vegetable mixture into a delicious soup. Serve with a mixed green salad and warm flour tortillas for a perfect weeknight dinner.

**ACTIVE TIME:** 24 MINUTES · **TOTAL TIME:** 45 MINUTES

**MAKES:** 4 MAIN-DISH SERVINGS

| | | | |
|---|---|---|---|
| 1 | TABLESPOON OLIVE OIL | 2 | CANS (15 TO 19 OUNCES EACH) BLACK BEANS, RINSED AND DRAINED, OR 3 CUPS HOME-COOKED BEANS, PAGE 10 |
| 1 | MEDIUM ONION, COARSELY CHOPPED | | |
| 1 | STALK CELERY, COARSELY CHOPPED | 1 | CAN (14½ OUNCES) VEGETABLE BROTH |
| 1 | MEDIUM CARROT, PEELED AND COARSELY CHOPPED | 2 | CUPS WATER |
| 1 | JALAPEÑO CHILE, SEEDS AND MEMBRANES DISCARDED, COARSELY CHOPPED | ½ | TEASPOON SALT |
| | | 2 | TABLESPOONS FRESH LIME JUICE |
| | | ½ | CUP LOOSELY PACKED FRESH CILANTRO LEAVES, CHOPPED |
| 2 | GARLIC CLOVES, MINCED | | |
| 1 | TEASPOON GROUND CUMIN | | LIME WEDGES AND NONDAIRY SOUR CREAM (OPTIONAL) |

**1** In 4-quart saucepan, heat oil over medium heat until hot. Add onion, celery, carrot, and jalapeño; cook until tender, about 10 minutes, stirring occasionally. Add garlic and cumin; cook 1 minute, stirring. Stir in beans, broth, water, and salt; heat to boiling over high heat. Reduce heat to low; simmer 15 minutes.

**2** Remove saucepan from heat. Following manufacturer's directions, use hand blender to puree mixture in saucepan until almost smooth. Stir in lime juice and sprinkle with cilantro. Serve with lime wedges and nondairy sour cream, if you like.

**EACH SERVING:** ABOUT 220 CALORIES | 12G PROTEIN | 43G CARBOHYDRATE | 5G TOTAL FAT (1G SATURATED) | 14G FIBER | 0MG CHOLESTEROL | 1,400MG SODIUM

# RED LENTIL AND VEGETABLE SOUP

This meal-in-a-bowl brims with fill-you-up soluble fiber, thanks to the lentils. Translation: It may help keep weight down and also helps lower total and "bad" LDL cholesterol.

**ACTIVE TIME:** 20 MINUTES · **TOTAL TIME:** 30 MINUTES

**MAKES:** 4 MAIN-DISH SERVINGS

| | | | |
|---|---|---|---|
| 1 | TABLESPOON OLIVE OIL | 1 | CAN (14½ OUNCES) VEGETABLE BROTH |
| 4 | MEDIUM CARROTS, PEELED AND CHOPPED | 2 | CUPS WATER |
| 1 | SMALL ONION, CHOPPED | ¼ | TEASPOON SALT |
| 1 | TEASPOON GROUND CUMIN | ⅛ | TEASPOON GROUND BLACK PEPPER |
| 1 | CAN (14½ OUNCES) DICED TOMATOES | 1 | BAG (5 OUNCES) BABY SPINACH |
| 1 | CUP RED LENTILS, RINSED AND PICKED THROUGH | | |

**1** In 4-quart saucepan, heat oil over medium heat until hot. Add carrots and onion; cook until tender and lightly browned, 6 to 8 minutes. Stir in cumin and cook 1 minute.

**2** Add tomatoes with their juice, lentils, broth, water, salt, and pepper; cover and heat to boiling over high heat. Reduce heat to low; cover and simmer until lentils are tender, 8 to 10 minutes.

**3** Just before serving, stir in spinach.

**EACH SERVING:** ABOUT 265 CALORIES | 16G PROTEIN | 41G CARBOHYDRATE | 5G TOTAL FAT (1G SATURATED) | 13G FIBER | 0MG CHOLESTEROL | 645MG SODIUM

# NOT YOUR GRANDMA'S BORSCHT

Your bubby's borscht was probably a hearty peasant-style stew, with chunks of beets, cabbage, and possibly some meat. Here we offer a leaner take on this Russian classic, boasting delicate grated beets and cabbage in a light vegetable broth, topped with a dollop of nondairy sour cream, if you choose. For photo, see page 94.

**ACTIVE TIME:** 15 MINUTES · **TOTAL TIME:** 1 HOUR 15 MINUTES
**MAKES:** 5 MAIN-DISH SERVINGS

| | | | |
|---|---|---|---|
| 1 | TABLESPOON OLIVE OIL | 4 | CUPS WATER |
| 1 | MEDIUM ONION, CHOPPED | 1 | CAN (14½ OUNCES) VEGETABLE BROTH |
| 1 | GARLIC CLOVE, CRUSHED WITH GARLIC PRESS | 1 | BAY LEAF |
| ½ | TEASPOON GROUND ALLSPICE | ¾ | TEASPOON SALT |
| 1 | CAN (14½ OUNCES) DICED TOMATOES | 2 | TABLESPOONS RED WINE VINEGAR |
| 1 | POUND (NOT INCLUDING TOPS) BEETS | ¼ | CUP LOOSELY PACKED FRESH DILL OR PARSLEY LEAVES, CHOPPED |
| 6 | CUPS SLICED GREEN CABBAGE (1 POUND) | | NONDAIRY SOUR CREAM (OPTIONAL) |
| 3 | LARGE CARROTS, PEELED AND CUT INTO ½-INCH PIECES | | |

**1** In 5- to 6-quart saucepot, heat oil over medium heat until hot. Add onion and cook until tender, about 8 minutes. Stir in garlic and allspice; cook 30 seconds. Add tomatoes with their juice and cook 5 minutes.

**2** Meanwhile, peel beets (see Tip) and shred in food processor or on coarse side of box grater.

**3** Add beets to onion mixture along with cabbage, carrots, water, broth, bay leaf, and salt; heat to boiling over high heat. Reduce heat to medium-low; cover and simmer until all vegetables are tender, about 30 minutes.

**4** Remove bay leaf. Stir in vinegar and dill. Serve with nondairy sour cream, if you like.

**TIP** It's impossible to peel beets without getting red beet juice all over your hands—unless you wear rubber gloves. Any kind will do: The juice washes right off them. For easy cleanup, peel beets in the sink.

**EACH SERVING:** ABOUT 160 CALORIES | 5G PROTEIN | 278G CARBOHYDRATE | 5G TOTAL FAT (1G SATURATED) | 6G FIBER | 0.5MG CHOLESTEROL | 920MG SODIUM

# CHINESE STIR-FRIED VEGETABLES WITH PASTA

Give your pasta an Asian spin with a sauce flavored with the spark of fresh ginger and the earthy goodness of soy sauce.

**ACTIVE TIME:** 20 MINUTES · **TOTAL TIME:** 30 MINUTES

**MAKES:** 4 MAIN-DISH SERVINGS

| | |
|---|---|
| 12 OUNCES CAPELLINI OR THIN SPAGHETTI | 1 TABLESPOON MINCED, PEELED FRESH GINGER OR 1 TEASPOON GROUND GINGER |
| 8 OUNCES SHIITAKE OR WHITE MUSHROOMS | ¼ CUP SOY SAUCE |
| 2 MEDIUM CARROTS, PEELED | 1 CAN (14½ OUNCES) VEGETABLE BROTH |
| 8 OUNCES SNOW PEAS | 1 CUP WATER |
| 1 TABLESPOON VEGETABLE OIL | ¼ TEASPOON CRUSHED RED PEPPER |

**1** Prepare pasta as label directs, but do not use salt in water. Drain.

**2** Remove tough stems from shiitake mushrooms or trim stem ends of regular mushrooms; slice mushrooms. Cut carrots into matchstick-thin strips. Remove stem and strings along edges of each snow pea.

**3** In 12-inch skillet, heat oil over medium-high heat until hot. Add ginger and mushrooms; cook until lightly browned. Stir in soy sauce and cook, stirring quickly and constantly, until mushrooms are tender and liquid is absorbed. Stir in carrots and snow peas; cook until tender-crisp, about 3 minutes.

**4** Add broth and water to skillet; heat to boiling over high heat. Stir in pasta; toss to coat well and heat through. Sprinkle with crushed red pepper and serve.

**EACH SERVING:** ABOUT 425 CALORIES | 14G PROTEIN | 80G CARBOHYDRATE | 5G TOTAL FAT (0.5G SATURATED) | 5G FIBER | 40MG CHOLESTEROL | 1,340MG SODIUM

# TOFU IN SPICY BROWN SAUCE

**We used a package of frozen Asian-style vegetables to make this super-fast dinner. For best quality, buy firm tofu sold in sealed packages.**

**ACTIVE TIME:** 15 MINUTES · **TOTAL TIME:** 20 MINUTES

**MAKES:** 6 MAIN-DISH SERVINGS

- 2 PACKAGES (16 OUNCES EACH) FIRM TOFU, DRAINED
- 1 CUP VEGETABLE BROTH
- ⅓ CUP REDUCED-SODIUM SOY SAUCE
- 1 TABLESPOON BROWN SUGAR
- 1 TABLESPOON CORNSTARCH
- 2 TABLESPOONS SEASONED RICE VINEGAR
- ⅛ TEASPOON CRUSHED RED PEPPER

- ½ CUP COLD WATER
- 1 PACKAGE (16 OUNCES) FROZEN ASIAN-STYLE VEGETABLES
- 1 TABLESPOON VEGETABLE OIL
- 3 GARLIC CLOVES, CRUSHED WITH GARLIC PRESS
- 2 TABLESPOONS MINCED, PEELED FRESH GINGER
- 3 GREEN ONIONS, SLICED STEAMED WHITE RICE (OPTIONAL)

**1** In 15 ½" by 10 ½" jelly-roll pan, place four layers paper towels. Cut each piece of tofu horizontally in half. Place tofu on towels in pan; top with four more layers paper towels. Gently press tofu with hand to extract excess moisture. Let stand 1 minute; repeat once, using more paper towels. Cut tofu into ½-inch pieces; set aside.

**2** In 2-cup glass measuring cup, with fork or wire whisk, combine broth, soy sauce, brown sugar, cornstarch, vinegar, crushed red pepper, and water, stirring until sugar and cornstarch are dissolved.

**3** In nonstick 12-inch skillet, heat frozen vegetables, covered, over medium heat 5 minutes, stirring occasionally. Uncover and cook until liquid evaporates, about 2 minutes longer, stirring occasionally. Transfer vegetables to bowl. Wipe skillet dry.

**4** In same skillet, heat oil over medium heat until hot. Add garlic and ginger; cook 1 minute. Stir broth mixture; add to skillet and heat to boiling over medium-high heat, stirring. Boil 1 minute. Stir in vegetables and tofu; cook until heated through, about 5 minutes. Sprinkle with green onions before serving. Serve with steamed rice, if you like.

**EACH SERVING:** ABOUT 295 CALORIES | 27G PROTEIN | 420G CARBOHYDRATE | 16G TOTAL FAT (2G SATURATED) | 4G FIBER | 0MG CHOLESTEROL | 870MG SODIUM

# JAPANESE EGGPLANT AND TOFU STIR-FRY

Japanese eggplant is long and slender. When cooked, it absorbs the wonderful flavor of the stir-fry sauce—serve with brown rice to get every drop.

---

**ACTIVE TIME:** 30 MINUTES · **TOTAL TIME:** 45 MINUTES PLUS STANDING

**MAKES:** 4 MAIN-DISH SERVINGS

---

1   PACKAGE (16 OUNCES) FIRM TOFU, DRAINED

½   CUP PLUS ⅓ CUP WATER

1   CUP VEGETABLE BROTH

¼   CUP REDUCED-SODIUM SOY SAUCE

2   TABLESPOONS BROWN SUGAR

2   TABLESPOONS CORNSTARCH

2   TABLESPOONS VEGETABLE OIL

4   MEDIUM JAPANESE EGGPLANTS (4 OUNCES EACH), CUT DIAGONALLY INTO 2-INCH PIECES

8   OUNCES SHIITAKE MUSHROOMS, STEMS REMOVED AND CAPS CUT INTO QUARTERS

1   TABLESPOON GRATED, PEELED FRESH GINGER

3   GARLIC CLOVES, CRUSHED WITH GARLIC PRESS

3   GREEN ONIONS, THINLY SLICED

2   HEADS BABY BOK CHOY (6 OUNCES EACH), CUT CROSSWISE INTO 1-INCH-THICK SLICES

**1**  In medium bowl, place four layers paper towel; add tofu and cover with four more layers paper towel, pressing lightly to extract liquid from tofu. Let tofu stand 10 minutes to drain, then cut into 1-inch cubes.

**2**  Meanwhile, in 2-cup liquid measuring cup, with fork or wire whisk, combine ½ cup water, broth, soy sauce, brown sugar, and cornstarch, stirring until brown sugar and cornstarch are dissolved; set aside.

**3**  In deep 12-inch skillet or wok, heat 1 tablespoon oil over medium-high heat until hot. Add eggplant and remaining ⅓ cup water; cover and cook until eggplant is tender, 7 to 10 minutes, stirring occasionally. Transfer eggplant to small bowl; set aside.

**4**  Add remaining 1 tablespoon oil to skillet and heat until hot. Add mushrooms and tofu; cook until tofu is lightly browned, about 5 minutes. Stir in ginger, garlic, and half of green onions; cook 1 minute, stirring. Add bok choy and cook until vegetables are lightly browned, about 4 minutes longer.

**5**  Stir broth mixture; add to tofu mixture with eggplant. Heat to boiling over medium-high heat; reduce heat to low and simmer 1 minute, stirring. Sprinkle with remaining green onions before serving.

---

**EACH SERVING:** ABOUT 280 CALORIES | 15G PROTEIN | 33G CARBOHYDRATE | 13G TOTAL FAT (1G SATURATED) | 5G FIBER | 0MG CHOLESTEROL | 865MG SODIUM

# SPICED PUMPKIN SOUP

This delicious soup delivers a double dose of antioxidants with the combination of pumpkin and carrots.

---

**ACTIVE TIME:** 20 MINUTES · **TOTAL TIME:** 45 MINUTES

**MAKES:** 8 CUPS OR 8 FIRST-COURSE SERVINGS

---

2 TABLESPOONS VEGAN STICK MARGARINE

1 MEDIUM CARROT, PEELED AND FINELY CHOPPED

1 MEDIUM ONION, FINELY CHOPPED

2 GARLIC CLOVES, MINCED

2 TEASPOONS GROUND CUMIN

½ TEASPOON GROUND CINNAMON

1 CARTON (32 OUNCES) VEGETABLE BROTH

1 CAN (29 OUNCES) SOLID PACK PUMPKIN (NOT PUMPKIN-PIE MIX)

1 CAN (12 OUNCES) CARROT JUICE

½ CUP HULLED PUMPKIN SEEDS (PEPITAS), ROASTED

**1** In 4-quart saucepan, melt margarine over medium heat. Add carrot and onion; cook until soft, 8 to 10 minutes, stirring frequently. Add garlic, cumin, and cinnamon; cook 1 minute, stirring. Add broth, pumpkin, and carrot juice to saucepan, stirring to combine. Cover and heat to boiling over high heat. Reduce heat to low; cover and simmer 15 minutes to blend flavors.
**2** Stir soup just before serving. Pass pumpkin seeds to sprinkle over soup.

---

**EACH SERVING:** ABOUT 190 CALORIES | 8G PROTEIN | 19G CARBOHYDRATE | 10G TOTAL FAT (2G SATURATED) | 5G FIBER | 0MG CHOLESTEROL | 570MG SODIUM

## VEGAN-WISE BUTTER ALTERNATIVES

If you're trying to cut back on cholesterol, then you might embrace the omission of butter that a vegan diet dictates. But if you find yourself yearning for the sweet fresh taste of butter, don't despair. Look for nonhydrogenated vegan margarines at the grocery store, sold in tubs for the table and in stick form for baking. These sweet and creamy spreads are just the thing when you need that buttery flavor in a soup, casserole, or baked good. That said, this book provides lots of creative ideas for avoiding butter and cutting back on oil, from using heart-healthy olive oil to substituting applesauce in baked goods to using just a spritz of cooking spray.

# MOROCCAN-SPICED SWEET POTATO MEDLEY

**This fragrant stew is both heart-healthy and satisfying.**

**ACTIVE TIME:** 15 MINUTES · **TOTAL TIME:** 45 MINUTES

**MAKES:** 4 MAIN-DISH SERVINGS

- 2 TEASPOONS OLIVE OIL
- 1 MEDIUM YELLOW ONION, CHOPPED
- 3 GARLIC CLOVES, CRUSHED WITH GARLIC PRESS
- 1½ TEASPOONS CURRY POWDER
- 1½ TEASPOONS GROUND CUMIN
- ¼ TEASPOON GROUND ALLSPICE
- 1 CAN (14½ OUNCES) DICED TOMATOES
- 1 CAN (14½ OUNCES) REDUCED-SODIUM VEGETABLE BROTH

- 1 CUP NO-SALT-ADDED GARBANZO BEANS, RINSED AND DRAINED
- 1 LARGE SWEET POTATO (1 POUND), PEELED AND CUT INTO ¾-INCH PIECES
- 2 SMALL ZUCCHINI (6 OUNCES EACH), CUT INTO ¾-INCH PIECES
- 1 CUP WHOLE-GRAIN COUSCOUS (MOROCCAN PASTA)
- ¼ CUP LOOSELY PACKED FRESH MINT LEAVES, CHOPPED

**1** In nonstick 12-inch skillet, heat oil over medium heat until hot. Add onion and cook until tender and lightly browned, 8 to 10 minutes, stirring occasionally. Stir in garlic, curry powder, cumin, and allspice; cook 30 seconds.

**2** Add tomatoes, broth, beans, and sweet potato; cover and heat to boiling over medium-high heat. Reduce heat to medium and cook 10 minutes.

**3** Stir in zucchini, cover, and cook until vegetables are tender, about 10 minutes.

**4** Meanwhile, prepare couscous as label directs.

**5** Stir mint into stew. Serve stew with couscous.

**EACH SERVING:** ABOUT 360 CALORIES | 14G PROTEIN | 70G CARBOHYDRATE | 5G TOTAL FAT (1G SATURATED) | 13G FIBER | 0MG CHOLESTEROL | 670MG SODIUM

# GINGERY CHICKPEA AND TOMATO STEW

The chickpea stew can be prepared up to two days ahead; transfer to an airtight container and refrigerate. The cilantro yogurt and rice are best prepared just before serving.

**ACTIVE TIME:** 15 MINUTES · **TOTAL TIME:** 40 MINUTES

**MAKES:** 4 MAIN-DISH SERVINGS

| | | | |
|---|---|---|---|
| 2 | TABLESPOONS VEGETABLE OIL | 1 | CAN (28 OUNCES) DICED TOMATOES |
| 1 | JUMBO ONION (1 POUND), CHOPPED | 2 | TABLESPOONS FRESH LEMON JUICE |
| 2 | GARLIC CLOVES, CRUSHED WITH GARLIC PRESS | 1 | TABLESPOON GRATED, PEELED FRESH GINGER |
| 1 | CUP BASMATI RICE | 3 | CUPS COOKED GARBANZO BEANS OR 2 CANS (15 OUNCES EACH) LOW-SODIUM GARBANZO BEANS |
| 1 | CUP NONDAIRY PLAIN YOGURT | | |
| ¼ | CUP PACKED FRESH CILANTRO LEAVES, FINELY CHOPPED | ½ | CUP WATER |
| 2 | TEASPOONS GROUND CUMIN | 1½ | TEASPOON SUGAR |
| 1 | TEASPOON GROUND CORIANDER | ¼ | TEASPOON SALT |
| ¼ | TEASPOON GROUND RED PEPPER (CAYENNE) | | PAPPADUMS (INDIAN FLATBREADS, OPTIONAL) |

**1** In 5- to 6-quart saucepot, heat oil over medium heat until hot. Add onion and garlic; cook 10 minutes or until golden and tender, stirring occasionally.

**2** Meanwhile, cook rice as label directs. In small bowl, combine yogurt and cilantro. Cover and refrigerate cilantro yogurt until ready to serve.

**3** To saucepot with onion, add cumin, coriander, and ground red pepper. Cook 1 minute or until fragrant, stirring. Add tomatoes, lemon juice, and ginger. Heat to boiling, then stir in garbanzo beans and water.

**4** Simmer 15 to 20 minutes or until sauce thickens, mashing a few beans and stirring occasionally. Stir in sugar and salt. Makes about 7 cups.

**5** Divide rice among dinner plates. Top with bean mixture and yogurt. Serve with pappadums, if you like.

**EACH SERVING:** ABOUT 485 CALORIES | 27G PROTEIN | 80G CARBOHYDRATE | 11G TOTAL FAT (1G SATURATED) | 14G FIBER | 0MG CHOLESTEROL | 900MG SODIUM

# COMFORT FOOD

This chapter is chock full of hearty fare sure to satisfy your family. If you're worried that giving up meat and cheese means giving up fun foods like pizza, burritos, and macaroni and cheese, you'll take comfort in the yummy versions offered in these pages. We consider an occasional dose of comfort food an essential part of every diet, and we invite you to indulge with gusto!

If you associate comfort food with something creamy and cheesy, then you'll be happy to know that vegan substitutes for many cheeses are now available at health-food stores and many large supermarkets. Our Macaroni and "Cheese" gets its satisfying creamy texture from a clever sauce made from soy Cheddar, vegan stick margarine, and silken tofu. And our Broccoli-"Cheese" Polenta Pizza is a healthful but delicious entrée featuring a precooked polenta base topped with a homemade almond ricotta and broccoli flowerets.

Stuffed vegetables are also a satisfying option for vegans craving a comfort food fix. We offer several recipes, including a stuffed acorn squash and bell peppers brimming with a bulgur and crumbled veggie burger stuffing. Hot from the oven, these dishes transform vegetables into an indulgence.

And, if you love takeout food, put down your phone and roll up your sleeves. We offer easy meat-free, dairy-free recipes for everything from fried rice to sesame noodles. You can have these dishes on your table, piping hot, long before the takeout guy would have shown up—and for a fraction of the cost!

*Fast-Fried Rice (page 126)*

# TOMATO AND RICE SOUP

Serve this comforting classic with crusty bread and a tossed salad for a satisfying winter meal. If you can't find either Wehani (an aromatic, reddish-brown rice that splits slightly when cooked and has a chewy texture) or black Japonica (a dark rice that tastes like a cross between basmati and wild rice), you can use long-grain brown rice.

**ACTIVE TIME:** 20 MINUTES · **TOTAL TIME:** 50 MINUTES
**MAKES:** 7½ CUPS OR 4 MAIN-DISH SERVINGS

| | | | |
|---|---|---|---|
| ½ | CUP WEHANI, BLACK JAPONICA, OR LONG-GRAIN BROWN RICE | 1 | CAN (28 OUNCES) WHOLE TOMATOES IN JUICE |
| 1 | TABLESPOON VEGAN STICK MARGARINE | 1 | CAN (14½ OUNCES) VEGETABLE BROTH |
| 1 | MEDIUM ONION, FINELY CHOPPED | ½ | TEASPOON SALT |
| 1 | MEDIUM STALK CELERY, FINELY CHOPPED | ¼ | TEASPOON COARSELY GROUND BLACK PEPPER |
| 1 | MEDIUM CARROT, PEELED AND CHOPPED | 1 | BAY LEAF |
| 1 | GARLIC CLOVE, CRUSHED WITH GARLIC PRESS | 1 | CUP WATER |
| ¼ | TEASPOON DRIED THYME | ½ | CUP LOOSELY PACKED FRESH PARSLEY LEAVES, CHOPPED |

**1**  Prepare rice as label directs but do not add salt or margarine. Set aside.

**2**  Meanwhile, in 4-quart saucepan, melt vegan margarine over medium heat. Add onion, celery, and carrot; cook until tender, about 10 minutes, stirring occasionally. Stir in garlic and thyme; cook 1 minute.

**3**  Add tomatoes with their juice, broth, salt, pepper, bay leaf, and water; heat to boiling over high heat, breaking up tomatoes with side of spoon. Reduce heat to medium-low and cook, covered, 30 minutes. Discard bay leaf.

**4**  Spoon one third of mixture into blender; cover, with center part of cover removed to let steam escape, and puree until almost smooth. Pour into large bowl. Repeat with remaining mixture.

**5**  Return soup to saucepan; heat over high heat until hot. Remove saucepan from heat; add cooked rice and chopped parsley.

**EACH SERVING:** ABOUT 190 CALORIES | 6G PROTEIN | 32G CARBOHYDRATE | 6G TOTAL FAT (3G SATURATED) | 4G FIBER | 0MG CHOLESTEROL | 960MG SODIUM

# JALAPEÑO CORNBREAD

What's not to love about a pan of homemade cornbread, hot from the oven? We gave this version some sass by throwing a chopped jalapeño into the batter.

ACTIVE TIME: 10 MINUTES · TOTAL TIME: 40 MINUTES
MAKES: 12 SERVINGS

| | |
|---|---|
| 1 CUP FROZEN CORN | 2 CUPS PLAIN UNSWEETENED SOY MILK |
| 2 CUPS CORNMEAL | 1 TABLESPOON APPLE CIDER VINEGAR |
| ¾ CUP ALL-PURPOSE FLOUR | ⅓ CUP CANOLA OIL |
| 1 TEASPOON BAKING POWDER | 2 TABLESPOONS AGAVE SYRUP |
| 1 TEASPOON BAKING SODA | 1 MEDIUM JALAPEÑO CHILE, SEEDED AND FINELY CHOPPED |
| ½ TEASPOON SALT | |

1  Preheat oven to 350°F. Line 13" by 9" baking pan with parchment paper and spray with nonstick cooking spray.

2  Rinse corn in colander with warm water to defrost. Drain thoroughly.

3  Meanwhile, in large bowl, sift together cornmeal, flour, baking powder, baking soda, and salt.

4  In medium bowl, whisk soy milk, vinegar, oil, and agave syrup until mixture begins to foam, about 1 minute. Pour wet ingredients into dry and stir until just combined. Fold in corn and jalapeño.

5  Pour into prepared pan, making sure batter is spread evenly. Bake for 30 to 35 minutes or until toothpick inserted in center comes out clean. Cut into 12 pieces.

**EACH SERVING:** ABOUT 220 CALORIES | 4G PROTEIN | 33G CARBOHYDRATE | 7G TOTAL FAT (0.5G SATURATED) | 2G FIBER | 0MG CHOLESTEROL | 270MG SODIUM

# BARLEY MINESTRONE

A bowlful of minestrone is always soothing. Top it with a dollop of our quick and easy pesto and you'll have comfort food that you can proudly serve to guests.

ACTIVE TIME: 50 MINUTES · TOTAL TIME: 1 HOUR 15 MINUTES
MAKES: 6 MAIN-DISH SERVINGS

| | | | |
|---|---|---|---|
| 1 | CUP PEARL BARLEY | 1 | GARLIC CLOVE, FINELY CHOPPED |
| 1 | TABLESPOON OLIVE OIL | 3 | CUPS WATER |
| 2 | CUPS THINLY SLICED GREEN CABBAGE (ABOUT ¼ SMALL HEAD) | 2 | CANS (14½ OUNCES EACH) VEGETABLE BROTH |
| 2 | LARGE CARROTS, PEELED, EACH CUT LENGTHWISE IN HALF, THEN CROSSWISE INTO ½-INCH-THICK SLICES | 1 | CAN (14½ OUNCES) DICED TOMATOES |
| | | ¼ | TEASPOON SALT |
| 2 | LARGE STALKS CELERY, CUT INTO ½-INCH DICE | 1 | MEDIUM ZUCCHINI (8 TO 10 OUNCES), CUT INTO ½-INCH DICE |
| 1 | MEDIUM ONION, CUT INTO ½-INCH DICE | 4 | OUNCES GREEN BEANS, TRIMMED AND CUT INTO ½-INCH PIECES (1 CUP) |
| | | | HOMEMADE PESTO (PAGE 116) |

1 Heat 5- to 6-quart Dutch oven over medium-high heat until hot. Add barley and cook until toasted and fragrant, 3 to 4 minutes, stirring constantly. Transfer barley to small bowl; set aside.

2 In same Dutch oven, heat oil over medium-high heat until hot. Add cabbage, carrots, celery, and onion; cook until vegetables are tender and lightly browned, 8 to 10 minutes, stirring occasionally. Add garlic and cook until fragrant, 30 seconds. Stir in barley, water, broth, tomatoes with their juice, and salt. Cover and heat to boiling over high heat. Reduce heat to low and simmer 25 minutes.

3 Stir zucchini and green beans into barley mixture; increase heat to medium, cover, and cook until all vegetables are barely tender, 10 to 15 minutes longer.

4 Meanwhile, prepare Homemade Pesto.

5 Ladle minestrone into 6 large soup bowls. Top each serving with a dollop of pesto.

**EACH SERVING:** ABOUT 215 CALORIES | 7G PROTEIN | 42G CARBOHYDRATE | 4G TOTAL FAT (0G SATURATED) | 9G FIBER | 0MG CHOLESTEROL | 690MG SODIUM

# VEGAN-WISE
## BARLEY BASICS

Barley is one of the oldest grains in cultivation. The fiber in barley may be even more effective than the fiber in oats at lowering cholesterol, so it's worth your while to work it into your diet.

**Pearl barley** has been polished (milled) to remove its outer hull, which omits some of the bran. It has a creamy, chewy texture. It's a great choice for soups, like the recipe opposite.

**Hulled barley** has had only the hull removed; it's chewier and more nutritious than pearl barley because it contains all of the bran but takes longer to cook. Use it as a base for stews or in casseroles.

# GRILLED PORTOBELLO AND TOMATO PANINI WITH HOMEMADE PESTO

Crusty ciabatta, fragrant grilled veggies, and homemade basil pesto—now that's a sandwich that deserves to be called comfort food!

TOTAL TIME: 15 MINUTES

MAKES: 4 SANDWICHES

### HOMEMADE PESTO

3 CUPS BASIL LEAVES

⅓ CUP PLUS 3 TABLESPOONS EXTRA-VIRGIN OLIVE OIL

¼ CUP WHOLE BLANCHED ALMONDS, TOASTED (SEE TIP)

2 SMALL GARLIC CLOVES

¼ TEASPOON SALT

¼ TEASPOON GROUND BLACK PEPPER

1 LOAF CIABATTA (1 INCH THICK)

4 LARGE PORTOBELLO MUSHROOMS, STEMS REMOVED

2 RIPE MEDIUM TOMATOES, SLICED ¼ INCH THICK

1  Pulse basil, ⅓ cup oil, almonds, and garlic in food processor until very finely chopped. Sprinkle in salt and pepper and pulse to combine.

2  Prepare outdoor grill for direct grilling over medium heat. Cut bread into four 4-inch by 4-inch pieces, and then split each horizontally in half so you have 8 pieces.

3  Brush mushrooms and tomatoes with 3 tablespoons oil and place on grill. Grill 6 to 8 minutes, turning over once. Transfer to plate.

4  Brush bread with oil and place on grill until slightly toasted, about 1 minute, flipping once. Transfer to plate.

5  Spread 1 tablespoon pesto on each piece of bread. On each of 4 pieces bread, layer 1 grilled mushroom and 3 slices tomato. Top with other half of bread. Cut each sandwich in half.

**TIP** To toast almonds, walnuts, or pecans, preheat oven to 350°F. Spread nuts in a single layer on a cookie sheet and bake, stirring occasionally, until lightly browned and fragrant, about 10 minutes.

**EACH SERVING:** ABOUT 480 CALORIES | 11G PROTEIN | 36G CARBOHYDRATE | 35G TOTAL FAT (5G SATURATED) | 5G FIBER | 2MG CHOLESTEROL | 403MG SODIUM

# SOUTH-OF-THE-BORDER BURRITO WRAPS

If you enjoyed a big beef burrito in your pre-vegan days, this wrap, which substitutes textured soy protein for the ground beef, is sure to satisfy.

ACTIVE TIME: 15 MINUTES · TOTAL TIME: 50 MINUTES

MAKES: 6 MAIN-DISH SERVINGS

1   CUP LONG-GRAIN BROWN RICE

2   MEDIUM CARROTS, PEELED AND CUT INTO 1-INCH PIECES

1   MEDIUM ONION, CUT INTO 1-INCH PIECES

1   MEDIUM STALK CELERY, CUT INTO 1-INCH PIECES

4   GARLIC CLOVES, PEELED

1   TABLESPOON OLIVE OIL

2   TABLESPOONS WATER

1   CAN (28 OUNCES) TOMATOES IN PUREE

1   POUND TEXTURED SOY PROTEIN

1¼ TEASPOONS GROUND CUMIN

½   TEASPOON SALT

2   TEASPOONS ADOBO SAUCE FROM CANNED CHIPOTLE CHILES OR 1 SMALL CANNED CHIPOTLE CHILE, MINCED

6   BURRITO-SIZE (10-INCH) WHOLE-WHEAT TORTILLAS, WARMED

ACCOMPANIMENTS:
SLICED ICEBERG LETTUCE, CHOPPED CILANTRO, CHOPPED GREEN ONIONS

1   Prepare brown rice as label directs; keep warm. Meanwhile, in mini food processor, with sharp side of blade facing up, pulse carrots, onion, celery, and garlic in batches until chopped (do not overprocess).

2   Heat oil in deep 12-inch skillet over medium-high heat until hot. Add chopped vegetable mixture and water, and cook until tender and golden, 15 to 20 minutes, stirring occasionally. Transfer vegetables to small bowl. Meanwhile, with kitchen shears, cut tomatoes, in their can, into bite-size pieces.

3   In same skillet, cook textured soy protein until it is browned and all liquid evaporates, about 10 minutes, breaking up clumps with side of spoon. Stir in cumin and salt, and cook 1 minute longer, stirring.

4   Return vegetable mixture to skillet with soy protein; stir in tomatoes with their puree and adobo sauce. Heat mixture to boiling over high heat. Reduce heat to low; cover and simmer until slightly thickened, about 10 minutes.

5   To serve, spoon about ½ cup rice down center of each warmed tortilla; top with about ¾ cup soy protein mixture. Sprinkle lettuce, cilantro, and green onion on top, if you like. Fold sides of tortillas over filling.

EACH SERVING: ABOUT 500 CALORIES | 23G PROTEIN | 61G CARBOHYDRATE | 18G TOTAL FAT (7G SATURATED) | 15G FIBER | 57MG CHOLESTEROL | 1,105MG SODIUM

# BROCCOLI-"CHEESE" POLENTA PIZZA

Here's a different flavor take on pizza, made with the toothsome corn goodness of ready-made polenta. See photo, opposite.

ACTIVE TIME: 20 MINUTES · TOTAL TIME: 25 MINUTES

MAKES: 4 MAIN-DISH SERVINGS

OLIVE OIL NONSTICK COOKING SPRAY

1 LOG (16 OUNCES) PRECOOKED PLAIN POLENTA, CUT INTO ¼-INCH-THICK SLICES

1 BAG (12 OUNCES) BROCCOLI FLOWERETS

¾ CUP ALMOND RICOTTA (OPPOSITE)

¼ CUP GRATED NONDAIRY PARMESAN SEASONING

1 TEASPOON FRESHLY GRATED LEMON PEEL

⅛ TEASPOON GROUND BLACK PEPPER

1 LARGE RIPE PLUM TOMATO (4 OUNCES), CHOPPED

1 Preheat broiler.

2 Coat 12-inch pizza pan or large cookie sheet with cooking spray. In center of pizza pan, place 1 slice polenta; arrange remaining slices in 2 concentric circles around first slice, overlapping slightly, to form a 10-inch round. Generously coat polenta with cooking spray. Place pan in oven about 4 inches from source of heat; broil polenta until heated through, about 5 minutes. Do not turn broiler off.

3 Meanwhile, in microwave-safe medium bowl, combine broccoli and 2 tablespoons water. Cover with plastic wrap, turning back one section to vent. Heat broccoli in microwave oven on High 3 minutes or just until tender. Drain.

4 In small bowl, combine Almond Ricotta, grated Parmesan, lemon peel, and pepper.

5 Arrange broccoli evenly over polenta. Drop cheese mixture by tablespoons over polenta and broccoli; sprinkle with tomato. Broil pizza until topping is hot, 3 to 5 minutes.

EACH SERVING: ABOUT 240 CALORIES | 11G PROTEIN | 27G CARBOHYDRATE | 11G TOTAL FAT (1G SATURATED) | 6G FIBER | 0MG CHOLESTEROL | 616MG SODIUM

# VEGAN-WISE
# ALMOND RICOTTA

This recipe delivers all the velvety goodness of ricotta without any dairy. We use it in Broccoli-"Cheese" Polenta Pizza opposite and in Whole-Wheat Pita Pizzas (page 47). But we're sure you'll find plenty of other delicious applications!

ACTIVE TIME: 3 MINUTES · TOTAL TIME: 5 MINUTES
MAKES: 1 CUP

½   CUP WHOLE BLANCHED ALMONDS
1½ CUPS WARM WATER
1   TABLESPOON LEMON JUICE

¼   TEASPOON SALT
1   TABLESPOON OLIVE OIL

1   Place almonds, water, lemon juice, salt, and oil in blender; blend until completely smooth, about 3 minutes.
2   Pour into medium saucepan. Heat to a simmer over medium heat; simmer until thickened, about 2 minutes, stirring frequently. Remove from heat and use as desired or cool and store in refrigerator.

**EACH SERVING (1 CUP):** ABOUT 545 CALORIES | 16G PROTEIN | 16G CARBOHYDRATE
50G TOTAL FAT (5G SATURATED) | 8G FIBER | 0MG CHOLESTEROL | 602MG SODIUM

# MACARONI AND "CHEESE"

**Here's everyone's favorite comfort food, vegan style.**

---

**ACTIVE TIME:** 5 MINUTES · **TOTAL TIME:** 15 MINUTES

**MAKES:** 7 CUPS OR 6 TO 8 SIDE-DISH SERVINGS

---

10 TO 12 OUNCES ELBOW MACARONI

1 PACKAGE (12 OUNCES) SILKEN TOFU

½ TEASPOON SALT

2 TABLESPOONS VEGAN STICK MARGARINE

1½ CUPS PACKED SHREDDED SOY CHEDDAR CHEESE

½ CUP PLAIN UNSWEETENED SOY MILK OR ALMOND MILK

**1** Cook macaroni as label directs, but do not add salt to water. Drain and set aside.

**2** Drain tofu and puree in food processor until completely smooth. Pour into medium saucepan and add salt, vegan margarine, soy Cheddar, and soy milk. Bring to a simmer over low heat, stirring frequently. Once hot, add macaroni and stir until heated through.

---

**EACH SERVING:** ABOUT 265 CALORIES | 14G PROTEIN | 33G CARBOHYDRATE | 7G TOTAL FAT (1G SATURATED) | 2G FIBER | 0MG CHOLESTEROL | 478MG SODIUM

## VEGAN-WISE
## THE SKINNY ON SOY CHEESE

If eliminating cheese from your diet feels like a sacrifice, take heart. Soy versions of many cheeses are now available, including cream cheese, Cheddar, grated Parmesan, Monterey Jack, and even feta. If you can't locate them at your local supermarket, check a health-food store or surf the web for online sources. Some versions are more convincing than others and flavor varies from brand to brand, so some experimentation is in order to find cheese substitutions you like. Typically, they don't melt as nicely as dairy cheese, but if you are hankering for cheese, you can find options that satisfy your craving.

# BULGUR AND VEGGIE STUFFED PEPPERS

For comfort food that's company fare, pack a rainbow of bell peppers with a stuffing that features bulgur and vegetable protein crumbles.

**ACTIVE TIME:** 20 MINUTES · **TOTAL TIME:** 1 HOUR 15 MINUTES
**MAKES:** 4 MAIN-DISH SERVINGS

4   LARGE RED, YELLOW AND/OR ORANGE PEPPERS WITH STEMS

1   CAN (14 TO 14.5 OUNCE) VEGETABLE BROTH

1¼ CUPS BULGUR

½   TABLESPOON OLIVE OIL

1   BUNCH GREEN ONIONS, CHOPPED

2   LARGE GARLIC CLOVES, CRUSHED WITH PRESS

1¼ CUPS VEGETABLE PROTEIN CRUMBLES

1   10-OUNCE PACKAGE FRESH SPINACH

¼   CUP FRESH MINT

1   CAN (28 OUNCES) CRUSHED TOMATOES

1   Cut ¾-inch slice from top of each pepper; reserve tops, including stems. Remove seeds and ribs, and cut a thin slice from bottom of each pepper so they will stand upright.

2   Arrange 4 peppers and their tops (separately) on same microwave-safe plate. Cook, uncovered, in microwave on High 4 minutes. With tongs, transfer pepper tops to paper towel. Microwave peppers 4 to 5 minutes longer, until just tender. Invert peppers onto paper towels to drain.

3   In large microwave-safe bowl, combine vegetable broth and bulgur. Cook, uncovered, in microwave on High for 12 to 15 minutes, or until bulgur is tender and most of the broth is absorbed.

4   Meanwhile, in deep 12-inch skillet, heat oil on medium until hot. Add garlic and onions; cook until garlic is fragrant but not cooked, about 2 minutes, stirring frequently. Add crumbles and sauté until heated through and beginning to brown, about 5 minutes. Remove skillet from heat.

5   Preheat oven to 350°F. Into skillet stir bulgur, 1 cup crushed tomatoes, spinach, and mint. Fill peppers with bulgur mixture, using a heaping cup for each. Replace pepper tops.

6   Pour remaining crushed tomatoes into 2-quart shallow casserole or 8" by 8" glass baking dish. Stir in salt and pepper. Place peppers in dish, standing up. Cover dish with foil and bake 35 minutes or until peppers are hot.

**EACH SERVING:** ABOUT 335 CALORIES | 21G PROTEIN | 70G CARBOHYDRATE | 4G TOTAL FAT (0.5G SATURATED) | 18G FIBER | 0MG CHOLESTEROL | 786MG SODIUM

# STUFFED ACORN SQUASH

Pine nuts and cannellini beans impart rich flavor and texture to this wild rice-stuffed acorn squash. The squash halves create natural bowls, so just grab a spoon and dig in.

ACTIVE TIME: 35 MINUTES · TOTAL TIME: 55 MINUTES

MAKES: 4 MAIN-DISH SERVINGS

2  ACORN SQUASH (1½ POUNDS EACH), CUT IN HALF AND SEEDED

1  TEASPOON OLIVE OIL

2  OUNCES VEGAN BACON, FINELY CHOPPED (OPTIONAL)

1  SMALL ONION (4 TO 6 OUNCES), FINELY CHOPPED

2  LARGE STALKS CELERY, FINELY CHOPPED

⅛  TEASPOON CRUSHED RED PEPPER

SALT AND GROUND BLACK PEPPER

1½  CUPS HOME-COOKED BEANS (PAGE 10) OR 1 CAN (15 OUNCES) LOW-SODIUM WHITE KIDNEY (CANNELLINI) BEANS, RINSED AND DRAINED

¼  CUP WATER

1  PACKAGE (7.4 OUNCES) HEAT-AND-SERVE PRECOOKED WILD RICE (DO NOT HEAT)

4  TEASPOONS PINE NUTS (PIGNOLI)

½  CUP PACKED FRESH BASIL LEAVES, THINLY SLICED

1  Preheat oven to 375°F. Line 15½" by 10½" jelly-roll pan with foil. On large microwave-safe plate, arrange squash halves in single layer, cut sides down. Microwave on High 9 to 11 minutes or until knife pierces flesh easily.

2  Meanwhile, in 12-inch skillet, heat oil over medium-high heat until hot. Add vegan bacon pieces and cook 3 to 4 minutes or until browned and crisp, stirring frequently. With spatula, transfer to paper towels to drain. Add onion, celery, crushed red pepper, ¼ teaspoon salt, and ¼ teaspoon pepper to skillet. Cook 4 to 5 minutes or until vegetables are tender and golden brown, stirring frequently. Remove from heat. In small bowl, mash ¼ cup beans with water. Into vegetables in skillet, stir rice, mashed beans, whole beans, vegan bacon, 2 teaspoons pine nuts, and half of basil. Season with salt and pepper to taste.

3  On prepared jelly-roll pan, arrange squash halves in single layer, cut side up. Divide bean mixture among squash cavities, pressing firmly into cavities and mounding on top. Cover pan with foil. Bake 15 minutes. Uncover and bake 5 to 7 minutes longer or until squash and vegetables are golden on top. Garnish with remaining pine nuts and basil.

EACH SERVING: ABOUT 320 CALORIES | 12G PROTEIN | 63G CARBOHYDRATE | 4G TOTAL FAT (0.5G SATURATED) | 11G FIBER | 0MG CHOLESTEROL | 346MG SODIUM

## SOMETHING NEW...
## STUFFED VEGETABLES

If you've been preparing vegan meals, you've probably steamed, sautéed, stir-fried, and roasted vegetables. But have you tried stuffing them? We offer recipes for filling acorn squash and bell peppers, but you can stuff all sorts of vegetables to the brim with other vegetables, whole grains, or some delectable combination. Portobello mushrooms, zucchini halves, and tomatoes are all good candidates. Just scoop out the seeds, brush with olive oil, fill and roast in a 375°F oven until the veggies have softened and the filling has browned.

# LO MEIN WITH TOFU, SNOW PEAS, AND CARROTS

Packaged ramen noodles can be a great short-cut ingredient. Here they're combined with tofu, snow peas, carrots, and bean sprouts for a tasty homemade lo mein.

**ACTIVE TIME:** 15 MINUTES

**MAKES:** 4 MAIN-DISH SERVINGS

2   PACKAGES (3 OUNCES EACH) ORIENTAL-FLAVOR RAMEN NOODLES

2   TEASPOONS VEGETABLE OIL

1   PACKAGE (16 OUNCES) EXTRA-FIRM TOFU, DRAINED, PATTED DRY, AND CUT INTO ¼-INCH PIECES

6   OUNCES (2 CUPS) SNOW PEAS, STRINGS REMOVED AND EACH CUT DIAGONALLY IN HALF

3   GREEN ONIONS, CUT INTO 2-INCH PIECES

1   PACKAGE (5 OUNCES) SHREDDED CARROTS (1½ CUPS)

½   CUP BOTTLED STIR-FRY SAUCE

3   OUNCES FRESH BEAN SPROUTS (1 CUP), RINSED AND DRAINED

**1**   Heat 4-quart covered saucepot of *water* to boiling over high heat. Add ramen noodles (reserve flavor packets) and cook 2 minutes. Drain noodles, reserving ¼ *cup cooking water*.

**2**   Meanwhile, in nonstick 12-inch skillet, heat oil over medium-high heat until very hot. Add tofu and cook until lightly browned, 5 to 6 minutes, gently stirring a few times. Add snow peas and green onions; cook until vegetables are tender-crisp, 3 to 5 minutes, stirring frequently. Stir in carrots, stir-fry sauce, and contents of 1 ramen flavor packet to taste (depending on salt level of sauce); cook until carrots are tender, about 2 minutes. (Discard remaining flavor packet or save for another use.)

**3**   Reserve some bean sprouts for garnish. Add noodles, reserved noodle cooking water, and remaining bean sprouts to skillet; cook 1 minute to blend flavors, stirring. Sprinkle with reserved bean sprouts to serve.

**EACH SERVING:** ABOUT 375 CALORIES | 18G PROTEIN | 47G CARBOHYDRATE | 12G TOTAL FAT (3G SATURATED) | 4G FIBER | 0MG CHOLESTEROL | 1,485MG SODIUM

# SOMETHING NEW...
# A GUIDE TO ASIAN NOODLES

**From udon to soba, Asian noodles make everyday dinners new. Here's an overview of inspiring options. If you can't find them at your local grocery store, visit an Asian market.**

**Udon noodles:** These wheat-based Japanese noodles are available fresh or dried. Fat and bouncy in texture, delicate fresh udon noodles cook fast, which makes them a great option for soups. Add to vegetable broth with tofu cubes, mixed vegetables, and a little miso for a quick, satisfying supper. Dried udon noodles are a great base for stir-fries; if you can't locate them, linguine is a good substitute.

**Soba noodles:** Soba are thin, delicately textured Japanese noodles made of buckwheat, which lends them a brown color and nutty flavor. They are traditionally served cold with a dipping sauce. Try them tossed with a store-bought peanut sauce. Top with chopped scallions.

**Chinese egg noodles**: These quick-cooking wheat-based noodles may be found in the produce section of the grocery store or in Asian markets. Because of the egg in the dough, they have a soft texture and rich flavor that creates a delicious base for any stir-fry you choose to top them with. Consider sprinkling some toasted chopped peanuts on top.

**Rice vermicelli:** These Southeast Asian noodles are made from dried rice flour. They have a mild flavor, and like white rice, they're perfect for soaking up the flavors of sauces—as in our Tofu Pad Thai, page 127—and broths. They can also be formed into cakes and pan-fried until crisp—a great way to dress up a simple stir-fry at a party.

# FAST-FRIED RICE

The secrets to this dish are quick-cooking brown rice, precut frozen vegetables, and ready-to-use stir-fry sauce. For photo, see page 110.

**TOTAL TIME:** 20 MINUTES

**MAKES:** 4 MAIN-DISH SERVINGS

1½ CUPS INSTANT (10-MINUTE) BROWN RICE

1 PACKAGE (16 OUNCES) FIRM TOFU, DRAINED AND CUT INTO 1-INCH CUBES

6 TEASPOONS OLIVE OIL

1 PACKAGE (16 OUNCES) FROZEN VEGETABLES FOR STIR-FRY

½ CUP BOTTLED STIR-FRY SAUCE

¼ CUP WATER

**1** In medium saucepan, prepare rice as label directs, but do not add salt to water.

**2** Meanwhile, place three layers of paper towels in medium bowl. Place tofu on towels and top with three more layers paper towels. Gently press tofu with hands to extract excess moisture.

**3** In nonstick 12-inch skillet, heat 2 teaspoons oil over medium-high heat until hot. Add frozen vegetables; cover and cook 5 minutes, stirring occasionally. Transfer vegetables to bowl; keep warm.

**4** In same skillet, heat remaining 4 teaspoons oil until hot. Add tofu and cook 5 minutes, gently stirring. Stir in rice and cook 4 minutes longer.

**5** Add stir-fry sauce, vegetables, and water; cook 1 minute, stirring. Serve immediately.

**EACH SERVING:** ABOUT 365 CALORIES | 16G PROTEIN | 44G CARBOHYDRATE | 15G TOTAL FAT (2G SATURATED) | 5G FIBER | 0MG CHOLESTEROL | 1,172MG SODIUM

# TOFU PAD THAI

Pad thai, Thailand's popular stir-fried noodle dish, is usually prepared with shrimp and scrambled eggs. Here we load up on green veggies and substitute tofu cubes for the eggs.

**TOTAL TIME:** 30 MINUTES PLUS SOAKING
**MAKES:** 4 MAIN-DISH SERVINGS

8 OUNCES RICE NOODLES (RICE VERMICELLI) OR 8 OUNCES ANGEL-HAIR PASTA

¼ CUP FRESH LIME JUICE

3 TABLESPOONS SOY SAUCE

2 TABLESPOONS SUGAR

2 TABLESPOONS WATER

1½ TO 2 TEASPOONS ASIAN CHILI OIL

2 LARGE GARLIC CLOVES, CRUSHED WITH GARLIC PRESS

1 POUND FIRM TOFU, DRAINED AND CUT INTO ½-INCH PIECES

4 CUPS SHREDDED CABBAGE FOR COLESLAW

⅓ CUP UNSALTED ROASTED PEANUTS, COARSELY CHOPPED

2 GREEN ONIONS, THINLY SLICED

1 In large bowl, soak rice noodles in enough *very hot water* to cover, 25 minutes. (If using angel-hair pasta, break in half and cook as label directs; rinse under cold water to stop cooking; drain.)

2 Meanwhile, in small bowl, combine lime juice, soy sauce, sugar, and water.

3 In nonstick 12-inch skillet, heat chili oil over medium-high heat until hot. Stir in garlic; cook 30 seconds. Add tofu and cook 1 minute or just until heated through, stirring frequently.

4 Drain rice noodles. Add noodles or angel-hair pasta to skillet and cook 2 minutes, stirring constantly. Add soy-sauce mixture, cabbage, and peanuts; cook 1 minute.

5 Transfer pad thai to bowls. Top with green onions.

**EACH SERVING:** ABOUT 435 CALORIES | 15G PROTEIN | 66G CARBOHYDRATE | 13G TOTAL FAT (1.5G SATURATED) | 4G FIBER | 0MG CHOLESTEROL | 706MG SODIUM

# SESAME NOODLES

A peanut butter and sesame dressing spiked with orange juice makes this Chinese restaurant–style pasta a favorite with kids as well as adults.

ACTIVE TIME: 15 MINUTES · TOTAL TIME: 30 MINUTES

MAKES: 6 MAIN-DISH SERVINGS

1   PACKAGE (16 OUNCES) SPAGHETTI

1   CUP FRESH ORANGE JUICE

¼   CUP SEASONED RICE VINEGAR

¼   CUP SOY SAUCE

¼   CUP CREAMY PEANUT BUTTER

1   TABLESPOON ASIAN SESAME OIL

1   TABLESPOON GRATED, PEELED FRESH GINGER

2   TEASPOONS SUGAR

¼   TEASPOON CRUSHED RED PEPPER

1   BAG (10 OUNCES) SHREDDED CARROTS (ABOUT 3½ CUPS)

3   KIRBY CUCUMBERS (ABOUT 4 OUNCES EACH), UNPEELED AND CUT INTO 2" BY ¼" MATCHSTICK STRIPS

2   GREEN ONIONS, TRIMMED AND THINLY SLICED

2   TABLESPOONS SESAME SEEDS, TOASTED (OPTIONAL)

GREEN ONIONS FOR GARNISH

1   In large saucepot, cook pasta as label directs but do not add salt to water.

2   Meanwhile, in medium bowl, with wire whisk or fork, mix orange juice, vinegar, soy sauce, peanut butter, sesame oil, ginger, sugar, and crushed red pepper until blended; set aside.

3   Place carrots in colander; drain pasta over carrots. In warm serving bowl, toss pasta mixture, cucumbers, and sliced green onions with peanut sauce. If you like, sprinkle pasta with sesame seeds. Garnish with green onions.

EACH SERVING: ABOUT 445 CALORIES | 15G PROTEIN | 7G CARBOHYDRATE | 9G TOTAL FAT (2G SATURATED) | 5G FIBER | 0MG CHOLESTEROL | 1,125MG SODIUM

# SAVORY & SWEET TREATS

If you are eating a completely dairy-free diet, or just attempting to cut back on dairy products, the biggest challenge may be locating an appropriate snack when you need one. This can mean that you'll fill up on junk food—potato chips, candy, even French fries in a pinch—none of which complement your efforts to consume nourishing meals filled with vegetables, beans, and whole grains during the rest of the day. We sympathize with this dilemma, and we are here to help.

This chapter delivers a roster of tasty vegan snacks and treats that you and your family members can reach for whenever you need a quick bite to tide you over until mealtime. It will take a little forethought and organization—you don't want to be whipping together hummus when you are completely ravenous—but we've provided lots of delicious recipes you can prepare and keep on hand in the fridge, at work or at home. And many of these snack foods are easy to pack: just fill up a zip-tight bag or plastic container and bring them on the road with you, wherever your days take you.

If you are hankering for a savory snack, our Cracked Wheat Pretzels or Hot-Pepper Nuts are easy to pack and pop into your mouth while you're on the go. Dip the pretzels in some peanut butter to add some protein to your break. We also provide a wide variety of dips—from guacamole to hummus to luscious Lemon-Cilantro Eggplant Dip. Add some carrot or celery sticks and you have a quick and easy snack that's as good for you as it is good tasting.

If you or the kids love sweets, fabulous options abound. Pack some Chocolate Chip–Walnut Brownies or Wheat-Free Almond Butter Cookies and you'll be prepared when the urge hits. Fruit is a good snack to reach for when you yearn for something sweet. From Chocolate-Dipped Banana Pops to Very Berry Granita, we have your options covered.

*Fruit Salsa with Cinnamon-Sugar Tortilla Chips (page 143)*

# THE SAVORY SNACKS

## HOT-PEPPER NUTS

If you like, use cashews, pecans, or almonds instead of walnuts. Just try not to eat them all; these make great gifts!

---

ACTIVE TIME: 5 MINUTES · TOTAL TIME: 30 MINUTES
MAKES: 2 CUPS

---

8   OUNCES WALNUTS (2 CUPS)

1   TABLESPOON VEGAN STICK
    MARGARINE, MELTED

2   TEASPOONS SOY SAUCE

½ TO 2 TEASPOONS HOT PEPPER SAUCE

1   Preheat oven to 350°F. Lightly grease jelly-roll pan.

2   In prepared jelly-roll pan, toss walnuts with melted butter until coated. Bake walnuts, stirring occasionally, until well toasted, about 25 minutes. Drizzle soy sauce and hot pepper sauce over nuts, tossing until well mixed. Cool completely in pan on wire rack. Store nuts in airtight container up to 1 month.

---

**EACH ¼ CUP:** ABOUT 211 CALORIES | 4G PROTEIN | 6G CARBOHYDRATE | 21G TOTAL FAT (3G SATURATED) | 2G FIBER | 4MG CHOLESTEROL | 116MG SODIUM

## CURRIED NUTS

Prepare nuts as directed above but substitute **1 teaspoon curry powder**, **½ teaspoon ground cumin**, and **½ teaspoon salt** for soy sauce and hot pepper sauce.

## CHILI NUTS

Prepare nuts as directed above but substitute **1 tablespoon chili powder** and **½ teaspoon salt** for soy sauce and hot pepper sauce.

## SWEET-AND-SPICY NUTS

Prepare nuts as directed above but substitute **2 tablespoons sugar**, **1½ teaspoons Worcestershire sauce**, **½ teaspoon ground red pepper** (cayenne), and **¼ teaspoon salt** for soy sauce and hot pepper sauce.

# CRACKED WHEAT PRETZELS

This is a great way to give your kids a double shot of whole-grain goodness at snack time. These crunchy pretzels are made with cracked wheat and whole-wheat flour.

ACTIVE TIME: 45 MINUTES · TOTAL TIME: 1 HOUR PLUS STANDING

MAKES: 12 PRETZELS

1 CUP BOILING WATER

¼ CUP CRACKED WHEAT (COARSE)

ABOUT 1½ CUPS ALL-PURPOSE FLOUR

1½ CUPS VERY WARM WATER (120°F TO 130°F)

1 PACKAGE QUICK-RISE YEAST

2 TEASPOONS SUGAR

1 TEASPOON TABLE SALT

1½ CUPS STONE-GROUND WHOLE-WHEAT FLOUR

1 TABLESPOON BAKING SODA

1 TEASPOON KOSHER SALT

1 In small bowl, pour boiling water over cracked wheat. Cover bowl with plastic wrap and let stand 30 minutes. Pour into a large sieve and drain.

2 In large bowl, combine all-purpose flour, 1¼ cups very warm water, yeast, sugar, and table salt; stir to dissolve. Stir in whole-wheat flour and drained cracked wheat. Mix well with wooden spoon. Knead dough until smooth and elastic, 4 to 6 minutes. Shape dough into ball; place in greased large bowl, turning dough over to grease top. Cover bowl and let rest 10 minutes.

3 Preheat oven to 400°F. Grease 2 large cookie sheets. Punch down dough and cut into 12 equal pieces. Roll each piece into a 20-inch-long rope. Shape ropes into pretzels and place 1½ inches apart on prepared cookie sheets. Let rise 10 minutes.

4 In small bowl, whisk remaining ¼ cup warm water with baking soda until soda dissolves. Brush baking soda mixture on pretzels and sprinkle with kosher salt. Bake pretzels, rotating sheets between upper and lower racks halfway through baking, until browned, 16 to 18 minutes. Transfer to wire racks to cool. Serve warm or at room temperature.

EACH PRETZEL: ABOUT 138 CALORIES | 5G PROTEIN | 28G CARBOHYDRATE | 1G TOTAL FAT (0G SATURATED) | 3G FIBER | 0MG CHOLESTEROL | 670MG SODIUM

# LEMONY HUMMUS

Middle Eastern dips such as hummus once seemed exotic, but now they've become familiar old friends. Of course you can buy hummus readymade at the grocery store, but making your own is so much more satisfying, not to mention economical. Tahini is readily available at health-food stores and supermarkets.

---

TOTAL TIME: 15 MINUTES PLUS CHILLING

MAKES: 2 CUPS DIP

---

- 4 GARLIC CLOVES, PEELED
- 1 LARGE LEMON
- 1 CAN (15 TO 19 OUNCES) GARBANZO BEANS, RINSED AND DRAINED
- 2 TABLESPOONS TAHINI (SESAME SEED PASTE)
- 3 TABLESPOONS OLIVE OIL
- 2 TABLESPOONS WATER
- ½ TEASPOON SALT
- ⅛ TEASPOON GROUND RED PEPPER (CAYENNE)
- ½ TEASPOON PAPRIKA
- 2 TABLESPOONS CHOPPED FRESH CILANTRO (OPTIONAL)

  TOASTED PITA BREAD WEDGES (OPTIONAL)

  OLIVES

1  In 1-quart saucepan, heat *2 cups water* to boiling over high heat. Add garlic and cook 3 minutes to blanch; drain.

2  From lemon, grate 1 teaspoon peel and squeeze 3 tablespoons juice. In food processor with knife blade attached, combine beans, tahini, blanched garlic, lemon peel and juice, oil, water, salt, and ground red pepper. Puree until smooth. Transfer to bowl; cover and refrigerate up to 4 hours.

3  To serve, sprinkle with paprika and cilantro, if using. Serve with pita bread wedges and olives.

---

**EACH TABLESPOON:** ABOUT 28 CALORIES | 1G PROTEIN | 2G CARBOHYDRATE | 2G TOTAL FAT (0G SATURATED) | 3G FIBER | 0MG CHOLESTEROL | 54MG SODIUM

# ROASTED RED PEPPER DIP

A tasty dip with a Middle Eastern accent. Serve with vegetables, pita chips, or spread it on a sandwich.

TOTAL TIME: 45 MINUTES

MAKES: 2 CUPS DIP

4   RED PEPPERS, ROASTED (SEE BELOW)

½   TEASPOON GROUND CUMIN

½   CUP WALNUTS, TOASTED

2   SLICES FIRM WHITE BREAD, TORN INTO PIECES

2   TABLESPOONS VINEGAR, PREFERABLY RASPBERRY

1   TABLESPOON OLIVE OIL

½   TEASPOON SALT

⅛   TEASPOON GROUND RED PEPPER (CAYENNE)

TOASTED PITA BREAD WEDGES

**1**  Cut roasted peppers into large pieces. In small skillet, toast cumin over low heat, stirring constantly, until very fragrant, 1 to 2 minutes.

**2**  In food processor with knife blade attached, process walnuts until ground. Add roasted peppers, cumin, bread, vinegar, oil, salt, and ground red pepper; puree until smooth. Transfer to bowl. If not serving right away, cover and refrigerate up to 4 hours. Serve with toasted pita bread wedges.

**EACH TABLESPOON:** ABOUT 23 CALORIES | 0G PROTEIN | 2G CARBOHYDRATE | 2G TOTAL FAT (0G SATURATED) | 0G FIBER | 0MG CHOLESTEROL | 46MG SODIUM

## ROASTED RED PEPPERS

**1**  Preheat broiler. Line broiling pan with foil. Cut each pepper lengthwise in half; remove and discard stems and seeds. Arrange peppers, cut side down, in prepared broiling pan. Place pan in broiler, 5 to 6 inches from heat source. Broil, without turning, until skin is charred and blistered, 8 to 10 minutes.

**2**  Wrap peppers in foil and allow to steam at room temperature 15 minutes or until cool enough to handle.

**3**  Remove peppers from foil. Peel skin and discard.

# LEMON-CILANTRO EGGPLANT DIP

The light, nutty flavor of tahini, an essential ingredient in hummus, pairs perfectly with rich roasted eggplant in this delicious Mediterranean dip. See photo, opposite.

---

ACTIVE TIME: 10 MINUTES · TOTAL TIME: 55 MINUTES PLUS CHILLING

MAKES: 2 CUPS DIP

---

2  EGGPLANTS (1 POUND EACH), EACH HALVED LENGTHWISE

4  GARLIC CLOVES, UNPEELED

3  TABLESPOONS TAHINI (SESAME SEED PASTE)

3  TABLESPOONS FRESH LEMON JUICE

¾  TEASPOON SALT

¼  CUP LOOSELY PACKED FRESH CILANTRO OR MINT LEAVES, CHOPPED

TOASTED OR GRILLED PITA BREAD WEDGES

CARROT AND CUCUMBER STICKS AND RED OR YELLOW PEPPER SLICES

1  Preheat oven to 450°F. Line 15½" by 10½" jelly-roll pan with foil and spray with nonstick cooking spray. Place eggplant halves, skin sides up, in foil-lined pan. Wrap garlic in foil and place in pan with eggplants. Roast 45 to 50 minutes or until eggplants are very tender and skin is shriveled and browned. Unwrap garlic. Cool eggplants and garlic until easy to handle.

2  When cool, scoop eggplant flesh into food processor with knife blade attached. Squeeze out garlic pulp from each clove and add to food processor with tahini, lemon juice, and salt; pulse to coarsely chop. Spoon dip into serving bowl; stir in cilantro. Cover and refrigerate at least 2 hours. Serve dip with toasted pita bread wedges and vegetables.

---

**EACH TABLESPOON:** ABOUT 10 CALORIES | 0G PROTEIN | 2G CARBOHYDRATE | 0G TOTAL FAT (0G SATURATED) | 1G FIBER | 0MG CHOLESTEROL | 55MG SODIUM

# EASY VEGAN CONDIMENTS
## NONDAIRY TZATZIKI DIPPING SAUCE

This Greek sauce is another great veggie dipper, or serve it on veggie burgers or in our Falafel Sandwiches (page 34). Tzatziki is typically made with yogurt; we swap in silken tofu for equally creamy results.

Peel and grate ½ **English cucumber**; place in a colander to drain. In a blender, puree the following until completely smooth: **1 cup silken tofu, 2 tablespoons olive oil, 2 teaspoons cider vinegar, 1 tablespoon lemon juice, ½ teaspoon salt**, and **¼ teaspoon pepper**. Transfer tofu mixture to a small bowl; add cucumber, pressing it first to make sure all water is drained. Holding a garlic press over the bowl, press **1 clove garlic**, then stir to combine. Refrigerate dip for at least 1 hour. Makes 1½ cups.

# TUSCAN WHITE-BEAN BRUSCHETTA

Bruschetta is toasted Italian bread that is rubbed with garlic and drizzled with olive oil. It's often topped with savory ingredients to make a simple appetizer or snack. Here we mash white beans with fresh sage, parsley, and lemon juice to create a version that's wholesome and delicious.

TOTAL TIME: 25 MINUTES

MAKES: 16 SERVINGS

1 LOAF (8 OUNCES) ITALIAN BREAD, CUT ON DIAGONAL INTO ½-INCH-THICK SLICES

8 GARLIC CLOVES, EACH CUT IN HALF

1 CAN (15 TO 19 OUNCES) WHITE KIDNEY BEANS (CANNELLINI), RINSED AND DRAINED, OR 1½ CUPS HOME-COOKED BEANS, PAGE 10

1 TABLESPOON FRESH LEMON JUICE

1 TABLESPOON OLIVE OIL

3 TEASPOONS CHOPPED FRESH PARSLEY

1 TEASPOON MINCED FRESH SAGE

¼ TEASPOON SALT

⅛ TEASPOON COARSELY GROUND BLACK PEPPER

1 Preheat oven to 400°F. Place bread slices on cookie sheet and bake until lightly toasted, about 5 minutes. Rub one side of each toast slice with cut side of garlic.

2 Meanwhile, in bowl, with fork, lightly mash beans with lemon juice. Stir in olive oil, 2 teaspoons parsley, sage, salt, and pepper.

3 Just before serving, spoon bean mixture over garlic-rubbed sides of toast slices. Sprinkle with remaining 1 teaspoon chopped fresh parsley.

**EACH SERVING:** ABOUT 35 CALORIES | 2G PROTEIN | 4G CARBOHYDRATE | 1G TOTAL FAT (0G SATURATED) | 2G FIBER | 0MG CHOLESTEROL | 77MG SODIUM

# KALE "CHIPS"

Our crisp kale "chips" are virtually fat free—perfect for guilt-free snacking.

---

ACTIVE TIME: 10 MINUTES · TOTAL TIME: 12 MINUTES

MAKES: 6 SERVINGS

---

1   BUNCH KALE (10 OUNCES), RINSED         ½ TEASPOON KOSHER SALT
    AND DRIED WELL

    NONSTICK COOKING SPRAY

Preheat oven to 350°F. From kale, remove and discard thick stems, and tear leaves into large pieces. Spread leaves in single layer on 2 large cookie sheets. Spray leaves with nonstick cooking spray to coat lightly; sprinkle with salt. Bake 12 to 15 minutes or just until crisp but not browned. Cool on cookie sheets on wire racks.

---

**EACH 1-CUP SERVING:** ABOUT 15 CALORIES | 1G PROTEIN | 3G CARBOHYDRATE | 0G TOTAL FAT (0G SATURATED) | 1G FIBER | 0MG CHOLESTEROL | 175MG SODIUM

# THE PERFECT GUACAMOLE

Our favorite avocados for guacamole are the varieties with thick, pebbly, green skin such as Hass, Pinkerton, and Reed. While guacamole is usually served as a dip, don't forget it's a great accompaniment for tacos or burritos or on top of a veggie burger.

**TOTAL TIME:** 15 MINUTES

**MAKES:** 1¾ CUPS DIP

1 JALAPEÑO CHILE, SEEDED AND FINELY CHOPPED

⅓ CUP LOOSELY PACKED FRESH CILANTRO LEAVES, CHOPPED

¼ CUP FINELY CHOPPED SWEET ONION SUCH AS VIDALIA OR MAUI

½ TEASPOON SALT

2 RIPE AVOCADOS

1 PLUM TOMATO

PLAIN TORTILLA CHIPS

1  In mortar, combine jalapeño, cilantro, onion, and salt; with pestle, grind until mixture becomes juicy and thick (onion can still be slightly chunky).

2  Cut each avocado lengthwise in half around seed. Twist halves in opposite directions to separate. Slip spoon between seed and fruit and work seed out. With spoon, scoop fruit from peel onto cutting board.

3  Cut tomato crosswise in half. Squeeze halves to remove seeds and juice. Coarsely chop tomato.

4  If mortar is large enough, add avocado and chopped tomato to onion mixture in mortar. (If mortar is small, combine avocado, tomato, and onion mixture in bowl.) Mash slightly with pestle or spoon until mixture is blended but still somewhat chunky.

5  Guacamole is best when served as soon as it's made. If not serving right away, press plastic wrap directly onto surface of guacamole to prevent discoloration and refrigerate up to 1 hour. Serve with chips.

**EACH TABLESPOON:** ABOUT 25 CALORIES | 0G PROTEIN | 1G CARBOHYDRATE | 2G TOTAL FAT (0G SATURATED) | 3G FIBER | 0MG CHOLESTEROL | 45MG SODIUM

# THE SWEET TREATS
## CANTALOUPE BOATS

Drizzle maple syrup and toasted almonds over raspberries, frozen yogurt, and sweet melon for a simple summer treat.

**TOTAL TIME:** 10 MINUTES

**MAKES:** 4 SERVINGS

¼   CUP SLICED ALMONDS

¼   CUP MAPLE SYRUP

1   RIPE MEDIUM CANTALOUPE (SEE TIP), CUT INTO QUARTERS, SEEDS REMOVED

1   PINT NONDAIRY VANILLA FROZEN YOGURT, SLIGHTLY SOFTENED

½   PINT RASPBERRIES

**1**   In small nonstick skillet, toast almonds over medium heat just until golden, stirring frequently. Remove skillet from heat and stir in maple syrup; set aside.

**2**   To serve, place cantaloupe quarters on 4 dessert plates. Top with non-dairy frozen yogurt, raspberries, and warm almond mixture.

**TIP** Once cut from the vine, a cantaloupe won't continue to ripen. It will soften, but its flavor won't improve, so it's important to buy one that is perfectly ripe. Pick a heavy melon in good shape, with no cracks or bruises. The blossom end should be smooth and the melon should be fragrant.

**EACH SERVING:** ABOUT 355 CALORIES | 5G PROTEIN | 50G CARBOHYDRATE | 14G TOTAL FAT (2G SATURATED) | 2G FIBER | 0MG CHOLESTEROL | 234MG SODIUM

# FRUIT SALSA WITH CINNAMON-SUGAR TORTILLA CHIPS

Here's a sweet take on a typically savory classic. The salsa is best made just before serving, but the homemade chips can be baked up to one week ahead. For photo, see page 130.

ACTIVE TIME: 25 MINUTES · TOTAL TIME: 35 MINUTES
MAKES: 3½ CUPS OR 8 SERVINGS

SWEET TORTILLA CHIPS

4 (8-INCH) FLOUR TORTILLAS

1 TABLESPOON VEGAN STICK MARGARINE, MELTED

1 TABLESPOON SUGAR

PINCH GROUND CINNAMON

SUMMER SALSA

1 LIME

1 TABLESPOON SUGAR

1 LARGE RIPE PEACH, PITTED AND CHOPPED

1 LARGE RIPE RED OR PURPLE PLUM, PITTED AND CHOPPED

1 LARGE RIPE APRICOT, PITTED AND CHOPPED

½ CUP DARK SWEET CHERRIES, PITTED AND CHOPPED

½ CUP SEEDLESS GREEN GRAPES, CHOPPED

1    Prepare Sweet Tortilla Chips: Preheat oven to 375°F.

2    Brush tortillas with vegan margarine. In cup, combine sugar and cinnamon. Sprinkle 1 side of each tortilla with cinnamon-sugar. Stack tortillas and cut into 6 wedges, making 24 wedges in total. Arrange wedges, sugar side up, in single layer on 2 large cookie sheets. Place on two oven racks and bake chips until golden, 10 to 12 minutes, rotating cookie sheets between upper and lower racks halfway through baking. Cool chips on cookie sheets on wire racks. Store chips in tightly covered container up to 1 week.

3    Just before serving, prepare Summer Salsa: From lime, grate ¼ teaspoon peel and squeeze 1 tablespoon juice. In medium bowl, stir lime peel, lime juice, sugar, and chopped fruit until combined.

4    To serve, spoon salsa into serving bowl. Use chips to scoop up salsa.

**EACH SERVING:** ABOUT 155 CALORIES | 3G PROTEIN | 28G CARBOHYDRATE | 4G TOTAL FAT (2G SATURATED) | 2G FIBER | 4MG CHOLESTEROL | 150MG SODIUM

# BANANA-BERRY PARFAITS

This layered dessert looks sensational served in an old-fashioned sundae glass. The ingredients are deliciously simple: nondairy vanilla yogurt, frozen raspberries, ripe bananas, plus just a little bit of sugar to sweeten the berries.

**TOTAL TIME:** 10 MINUTES

**MAKES:** 4 SERVINGS

---

1¼ CUPS UNSWEETENED FROZEN RASPBERRIES, PARTIALLY THAWED

1 TABLESPOON SUGAR

2⅔ CUPS NONDAIRY VANILLA YOGURT

2 RIPE BANANAS, PEELED AND THINLY SLICED

FRESH RASPBERRIES FOR GARNISH (OPTIONAL)

---

1 In food processor with knife blade attached, pulse thawed raspberries and sugar until almost smooth.

2 Into four 10-ounce glasses or goblets, layer about half of raspberry puree, half of yogurt, and half of banana slices; repeat layering. Top with fresh raspberries, if you like.

---

**EACH SERVING:** ABOUT 210 CALORIES | 5G PROTEIN | 43G CARBOHYDRATE | 3G TOTAL FAT (0G SATURATED) | 4G FIBER | 0MG CHOLESTEROL | 18MG SODIUM

# SUMMER FRUIT IN SPICED SYRUP

This is the perfect sweet ending to a backyard cookout. Serve it as is or spooned over nondairy vanilla ice cream or pound cake.

ACTIVE TIME: 15 MINUTES · TOTAL TIME: 25 MINUTES PLUS CHILLING

MAKES: 5 TO 6 CUPS OR 4 SERVINGS

| | | | |
|---|---|---|---|
| ¾ | CUP WATER | 1 | STRIP (3" BY ¾") LEMON PEEL |
| ½ | CUP SUGAR | 2 | TABLESPOONS FRESH LEMON JUICE |
| 3 | WHOLE CLOVES | 6 | CUPS FRESH FRUIT, SUCH AS SLICED NECTARINES, PLUMS, STRAWBERRIES, BLUEBERRIES, AND/OR RASPBERRIES |
| 1 | CINNAMON STICK (3 INCHES) | | |
| 1 | STAR ANISE | | |

1 In 1-quart saucepan, combine water, sugar, cloves, cinnamon stick, star anise, and lemon peel; heat to boiling over medium-high heat, stirring frequently. Reduce heat to medium-low; simmer 5 minutes.

2 Remove saucepan from heat; stir in lemon juice. Cool syrup to room temperature.

3 In large bowl, combine fruits and spiced syrup. Cover and refrigerate 2 hours, stirring occasionally.

**EACH SERVING:** ABOUT 125 CALORIES | 1G PROTEIN | 32G CARBOHYDRATE | 12G TOTAL FAT (0G SATURATED) | 4G FIBER | 0MG CHOLESTEROL | 2MG SODIUM

# VERY BERRY GRANITA

We love using raspberries or blackberries in this granita, but you can use blueberries or a combination of berries, if you like.

ACTIVE TIME: 15 MINUTES · TOTAL TIME: 20 MINUTES PLUS COOLING AND FREEZING
MAKES: 8 CUPS OR 16 SERVINGS

| | |
|---|---|
| 1   CUP SUGAR | 6   CUPS RASPBERRIES OR BLACKBERRIES |
| 1¼ CUPS WATER | 2   TABLESPOONS FRESH LIME JUICE |

1   In 2-quart saucepan, combine sugar and water; heat to boiling over high heat, stirring until sugar has dissolved. Reduce heat to medium and cook 1 minute. Set saucepan in bowl of ice water until syrup is cool.
2   Meanwhile, in blender or in food processor with knife blade attached, puree raspberries until smooth. With spoon, press puree through sieve into medium bowl; discard seeds.
3   Stir sugar syrup and lime juice into puree; pour into 8-inch square metal baking pan. Cover and freeze until partially frozen, about 2 hours. Stir with fork to break up chunks. Cover and freeze until completely frozen, at least 3 hours or up to overnight. To serve, let stand at room temperature until slightly softened, about 15 minutes. Use a metal spoon to scrape across the surface of the granita, transferring ice shards to chilled dessert dishes or wine goblets without packing them.

EACH SERVING: ABOUT 70 CALORIES | 0G PROTEIN | 18G CARBOHYDRATE | 0G TOTAL FAT ( 0G SATURATED) | 2G FIBER | 0MG CHOLESTEROL | 0MG SODIUM

## WATERMELON GRANITA

Prepare syrup as directed in Step 1, but use **¾ cup water**. Remove rind and seeds from **1 piece (5½ pounds) watermelon**; cut fruit into bite-size pieces (9 cups). In blender or in food processor with knife blade attached, in batches, puree watermelon until smooth. Press through sieve into large bowl; discard fibers. Stir sugar syrup and lime juice into watermelon puree. Freeze as directed. Makes about 9 cups or 18 servings.

EACH SERVING: ABOUT 70 CALORIES, 0G PROTEIN, 17G CARBOHYDRATE, 0G TOTAL FAT (0G SATURATED), 0G FIBER, 0MG CHOLESTEROL, 2MG SODIUM

# STUFFED FRESH FIGS

Figs are a good source of dietary fiber and potassium—and did we mention they're delicious? When you're lucky enough to find ripe figs in your market, be sure to try this recipe.

TOTAL TIME: 25 MINUTES

MAKES: 6 SERVINGS

19  SMALL FRESH RIPE FIGS (1¼ POUNDS; SEE TIP)

¼  CUP MAPLE SYRUP

½  CUP ALMOND RICOTTA (PAGE 119)

¼  CUP NATURAL ALMONDS, TOASTED (SEE TIP, PAGE 116) AND CHOPPED

1   On plate, with fork, mash ripest fig with maple syrup; set aside.

2   With sharp knife, trim stems from remaining figs, then cut a deep X in the top of each, making sure not to cut all the way through to bottom. With fingertips, gently spread each fig apart to make "petals."

3   In small bowl, combine Almond Ricotta and almonds. With back of spoon, press mashed fig mixture through sieve into 1-cup measure.

4   To serve, spoon ricotta mixture into figs. Arrange figs on platter. Drizzle with fig maple syrup.

**TIP** The season for fresh figs is short and they're expensive, so if you indulge in them, be sure to get your money's worth. Buy fruit that is heavy, smells fresh (not musty), and is soft to the touch. Use them promptly; figs will keep, refrigerated, for only a day or two. Rinse figs gently before using them. The entire fruit is edible, skin and all—just discard the stem.

**EACH SERVING:** ABOUT 185 CALORIES | 3G PROTEIN | 30G CARBOHYDRATE | 7G TOTAL FAT (1G SATURATED) | 4G FIBER | 0MG CHOLESTEROL | 52MG SODIUM

# CHOCOLATE-DIPPED BANANA POPS

**Bananas make a sumptuous low-fat base for these frozen pops.**

**TOTAL TIME:** 20 MINUTES PLUS FREEZING
**MAKES:** 12 POPS

12 (4-INCH) ICE-CREAM-BAR STICKS

4 LARGE RIPE BUT FIRM BANANAS, PEELED AND CUT CROSSWISE INTO THIRDS

1 PACKAGE (6 OUNCES) VEGAN CHOCOLATE CHIPS

2 TABLESPOONS VEGETABLE OIL

1 CUP CHOICE OF TOPPINGS (TOASTED SWEETENED FLAKED COCONUT, CHOPPED SALTED PEANUTS, AND/OR COLORED CANDY DECORS)

**1** Line cookie sheet with waxed paper. Insert ice-cream-bar stick, about 1 inch deep, in one end of each banana piece; place on cookie sheet.

**2** In small heavy saucepan, heat chocolate chips with oil over low heat until chocolate melts and becomes smooth, stirring occasionally. Place each topping on separate sheet of waxed paper.

**3** Holding 1 banana pop over saucepan, spoon some chocolate mixture over pop to coat, allowing chocolate to drip back into pan. Roll chocolate-coated banana in toppings. Return pop to cookie sheet. Repeat with remaining bananas, chocolate, and toppings. Freeze at least 1 hour.

**4** To serve, let pops stand at room temperature 5 minutes to soften slightly.

**EACH SERVING:** ABOUT 185 CALORIES | 1G PROTEIN | 27G CARBOHYDRATE | 9G TOTAL FAT (3G SATURATED) | 1G FIBER | 7MG CHOLESTEROL | 60MG SODIUM

# VEGAN-WISE
## A GUIDE TO CHOCOLATE

Is chocolate vegan? Some types are, some aren't. Obviously, milk chocolate isn't, ever. White chocolate (which technically isn't a chocolate because it doesn't contain cocoa solids) isn't. Unsweetened cocoa and unsweetened chocolate always are. When you get to semisweet and bittersweet chocolate, it depends. The only way you can be sure is to read the package. If the chocolate includes milk solids, it has to say so.

# CHOCOLATE CHIP–WALNUT BROWNIES

Don't be put off by the presence of prunes in this recipe—when going egg-free, fruit purees are often used to provide moistness and that satisfying unctuousness you get from eggs. The triple shot of cocoa, unsweetened chocolate, and chocolate chips will please any chocoholic.

**ACTIVE TIME:** 25 MINUTES · **TOTAL TIME:** 55 MINUTES
**MAKES:** 16 BROWNIES

| | |
|---|---|
| ⅔ CUP WATER | 3 OUNCES UNSWEETENED CHOCOLATE, MELTED AND COOLED |
| ⅓ CUP PITTED PRUNES | ⅓ CUP CANOLA OIL |
| 1 CUP ALL-PURPOSE FLOUR | 2 TEASPOONS VANILLA EXTRACT |
| 1 TEASPOON BAKING POWDER | 1⅓ CUPS SUGAR |
| ½ TEASPOON SALT | ¾ CUP WALNUTS, CHOPPED |
| ¼ TEASPOON BAKING SODA | ⅓ CUP VEGAN CHOCOLATE CHIPS |
| ⅓ CUP QUICK-COOKING OATS | |
| ¼ CUP UNSWEETENED COCOA | |

1   Preheat oven to 350°F. Line 9-inch square baking pan with foil; spray foil with nonstick cooking spray. Place water and prunes in microwave-safe bowl. Microwave on High 2 minutes. Let stand 5 minutes.

2   Meanwhile, in small bowl, whisk flour, baking powder, salt, and baking soda.

3   In food processor, process oats until finely ground. Add prunes and soaking water and process until very smooth, about 1 minute. Add cocoa and process until smooth.

4   Scrape prune mixture into large bowl. Stir in chocolate, oil, and vanilla until smooth. Add sugar and stir until well blended. Stir in flour mixture and then walnuts and chocolate chips. Scrape batter into prepared pan.

5   Bake until toothpick inserted in center comes out with moist but not wet crumbs, 30 to 35 minutes. Let cool completely on wire rack. To serve, remove from pan using foil, and cut into 16 squares.

**EACH BROWNIE:** ABOUT 235 CALORIES | 3G PROTEIN | 32G CARBOHYDRATE | 12G TOTAL FAT (3G SATURATED) | 3G FIBER | 0MG CHOLESTEROL | 136MG SODIUM

# DEEP CHOCOLATE CUPCAKES

When buying your bittersweet chocolate, be sure to read the package labels. Not all bittersweet (or semisweet) chocolates are created equal, and some include milk solids. Most premium brands don't—but check the package.

ACTIVE TIME: 25 MINUTES · TOTAL TIME: 45 MINUTES

MAKES: 12 CUPCAKES

### CUPCAKES

1½ CUPS ALL-PURPOSE FLOUR

¾ CUP GRANULATED SUGAR

⅓ CUP UNSWEETENED COCOA, SIFTED

¾ TEASPOON BAKING SODA

½ TEASPOON SALT

1 CUP COLD WATER

⅓ CUP CANOLA OIL

1 TABLESPOON CIDER VINEGAR

1½ TEASPOONS VANILLA EXTRACT

### FROSTING

1½ CUPS CONFECTIONERS' SUGAR

3 TABLESPOONS VEGAN STICK MARGARINE

1 TO 2 TABLESPOONS PLAIN SOY MILK

½ TEASPOON VANILLA EXTRACT

3 OUNCES VEGAN BITTERSWEET CHOCOLATE, MELTED AND COOLED

**1** Prepare cupcakes: Preheat oven to 350°F. Line 12-cup muffin pan with paper liners.

**2** In large bowl, whisk flour, granulated sugar, cocoa, baking soda, and salt until blended. Add water, oil, vinegar, and vanilla; whisk until batter is smooth. Spoon batter evenly into muffin cups. Bake until toothpick inserted in center of cupcakes comes out clean, 20 to 25 minutes. Remove cupcakes to wire rack to cool completely.

**3** Meanwhile, prepare frosting: In medium bowl, beat confectioners' sugar, vegan margarine, 1 tablespoon soy milk, and vanilla until smooth. Beat in chocolate until frosting is light and fluffy, adding remaining soy milk as needed to achieve easy spreading consistency. Spread frosting on cupcakes.

**EACH CUPCAKE:** ABOUT 285 CALORIES | 3G PROTEIN | 45G CARBOHYDRATE | 12G TOTAL FAT (3G SATURATED) | 2G FIBER | 0MG CHOLESTEROL | 208MG SODIUM

# OATMEAL-RAISIN COOKIES

When making these cookies, be sure to use vegan stick margarine, not spread (which has a lower fat content), or your cookie dough won't have the right consistency.

ACTIVE TIME: 35 MINUTES · TOTAL TIME: 1 HOUR

MAKES: 3 DOZEN COOKIES

| | | | |
|---|---|---|---|
| 1 | CUP ALL-PURPOSE FLOUR | ⅓ | CUP GRANULATED SUGAR |
| 1 | TEASPOON GROUND CINNAMON | ½ | CUP PLAIN SOY MILK |
| ½ | TEASPOON BAKING SODA | 1 | TEASPOON VANILLA EXTRACT |
| ½ | TEASPOON SALT | 3 | CUPS OLD-FASHIONED OATS |
| ¾ | CUP VEGAN STICK MARGARINE | 1 | CUP RAISINS |
| ¾ | CUP PACKED BROWN SUGAR | 1 | CUP WALNUTS, CHOPPED |

1  Preheat oven to 350°F. Spray 3 large baking sheets with nonstick cooking spray. In small bowl, whisk flour, cinnamon, baking soda, and salt.

2  In large bowl, beat vegan margarine, brown sugar, and granulated sugar until smooth and fluffy. Beat in soy milk and vanilla (it will look curdled; that's okay). Beat in flour mixture. Stir in oats, raisins, and walnuts.

3  Drop dough by heaping tablespoons onto prepared baking sheets, 2 inches apart. Bake one sheet at a time until cookies look dry and are browned at edges, 13 to 15 minutes. Let stand on baking sheet 1 minute before removing with wide spatula to wire rack to cool completely.

**EACH COOKIE:** ABOUT 135 CALORIES | 2G PROTEIN | 18G CARBOHYDRATE | 6G TOTAL FAT (2G SATURATED) | 9G FIBER | 0MG CHOLESTEROL | 93MG SODIUM

# WHEAT-FREE ALMOND BUTTER COOKIES

Food allergies are on the rise, so sometimes those who are lactose intolerant also discover they can't eat wheat gluten. Here's a sweet treat that will satisfy both limitations.

ACTIVE TIME: 10 MINUTES · TOTAL TIME: 25 MINUTES
MAKES: 3 DOZEN COOKIES

1 TABLESPOON GROUND FLAXSEEDS OR FLAXSEED MEAL

3 TABLESPOONS WATER

1 CUP SMOOTH ALMOND BUTTER

1 CUP PACKED BROWN SUGAR

1 TEASPOON BAKING SODA

½ TEASPOON VANILLA EXTRACT

PINCH SALT

½ TEASPOON PUMPKIN PIE SPICE (OPTIONAL)

SLICED ALMONDS (OPTIONAL)

1 Preheat oven to 350°F. Line two baking sheets with parchment paper.

2 In small bowl, mix flaxseeds with water. Let stand 5 minutes.

3 In electric mixer, combine almond butter, brown sugar, baking soda, vanilla, salt, soaked flaxseeds, and pumpkin pie spice if using; mix on low until thoroughly combined. Using a 1-tablespoon measure, form dough into balls and place on prepared baking sheets, 1½ inches apart. If desired, top balls with almonds.

4 Bake 11 to 12 minutes or until slightly golden. Cool on rack.

**EACH SERVING:** ABOUT 70 CALORIES | 1G PROTEIN | 8G CARBOHYDRATE | 4G TOTAL FAT (0.5G SATURATED) | 13G FIBER | 0MG CHOLESTEROL | 72MG SODIUM

# INDEX

# PHOTOGRAPHY CREDITS

# METRIC EQUIVALENTS CHARTS

The recipes that appear in this cookbook use the standard United States method for measuring liquid and dry or solid ingredients (teaspoons, tablespoons, and cups). The information on this chart is provided to help cooks outside the U.S. successfully use these recipes. All equivalents are approximate.

## METRIC EQUIVALENTS FOR DIFFERENT TYPES OF INGREDIENTS

A standard cup measure of a dry or solid ingredient will vary in weight depending on the type of ingredient. A standard cup of liquid is the same volume for any type of liquid. Use the following chart when converting standard cup measures to grams (weight) or milliliters (volume).

| Standard Cup | Fine Powder (e.g. flour) | Grain (e.g. rice) | Granular (e.g. sugar) | Liquid Solids (e.g. butter) | Liquid (e.g. milk) |
|---|---|---|---|---|---|
| 1 | 140 g | 150 g | 190 g | 200 g | 240 ml |
| ¾ | 105 g | 113 g | 143 g | 150 g | 180 ml |
| ⅔ | 93 g | 100 g | 125 g | 133 g | 160 ml |
| ½ | 70 g | 75 g | 95 g | 100 g | 120 ml |
| ⅓ | 47 g | 50 g | 63 g | 67 g | 80 ml |
| ¼ | 35 g | 38 g | 48 g | 50 g | 60 ml |
| ⅛ | 18 g | 19 g | 24 g | 25 g | 30 ml |

## USEFUL EQUIVALENTS FOR LIQUID INGREDIENTS BY VOLUME

| ¼ tsp | = | | | | | 1 ml |
|---|---|---|---|---|---|---|
| ½ tsp | = | | | | | 2 ml |
| 1 tsp | = | | | | | 5 ml |
| 3 tsp | = | 1 tbls | = | | ½ fl oz | = | 15 ml |
| | | 2 tbls | = | ⅛ cup | = | 1 fl oz | = | 30 ml |
| | | 4 tbls | = | ¼ cup | = | 2 fl oz | = | 60 ml |
| | | 5⅓ tbls | = | ⅓ cup | = | 3 fl oz | = | 80 ml |
| | | 8 tbls | = | ½ cup | = | 4 fl oz | = | 120 ml |
| | | 10⅔ tbls | = | ⅔ cup | = | 5 fl oz | = | 160 ml |
| | | 12 tbls | = | ¾ cup | = | 6 fl oz | = | 180 ml |
| | | 16 tbls | = | 1 cup | = | 8 fl oz | = | 240 ml |
| | | 1 pt | = | 2 cups | = | 16 fl oz | = | 480 ml |
| | | 1 qt | = | 4 cups | = | 32 fl oz | = | 960 ml |
| | | | | | | 33 fl oz | = | 1000 ml | = 1 L |

## USEFUL EQUIVALENTS FOR DRY INGREDIENTS BY WEIGHT
(To convert ounces to grams, multiply the number of ounces by 30.)

| 1 oz | = | 1/16 lb | = | 30 g |
|---|---|---|---|---|
| 2 oz | = | ¼ lb | = | 120 g |
| 4 oz | = | ½ lb | = | 240 g |
| 8 oz | = | ¾ lb | = | 360 g |
| 16 oz | = | 1 lb | = | 480 g |

## USEFUL EQUIVALENTS LENGTH
(To convert inches to centimeters, multiply the number of inches by 2.5.)

| 1 in = | | 2.5 cm |
|---|---|---|
| 6 in = | ½ ft = | 15 cm |
| 12 in = | 1 ft = | 30 cm |
| 36 in = | 3 ft = 1 yd | = 90 cm |
| 40 in = | | 100 cm = 1 m |

## USEFUL EQUIVALENTS FOR COOKING/OVEN TEMPERATURES

| | Fahrenheit | Celsius | Gas Mark |
|---|---|---|---|
| Freeze Water | 32° F | 0° C | |
| Room Temperature | 68° F | 20° C | |
| Boil Water | 212° F | 100° C | |
| Bake | 325° F | 160° C | 3 |
| | 350° F | 180° C | 4 |
| | 375° F | 190° C | 5 |
| | 400° F | 200° C | 6 |
| | 425° F | 220° C | 7 |
| | 450° F | 230° C | 8 |
| Broil | | | Grill |

# THE GOOD HOUSEKEEPING TRIPLE-TEST PROMISE

At *Good Housekeeping*, we want to make sure that every recipe we print works in any oven, with any brand of ingredient, no matter what. That's why, in our test kitchens at the **Good Housekeeping Research Institute,** we go all out: We test each recipe at least three times—and, often, several more times after that.

When a recipe is first developed, one member of our team prepares the dish and we judge it on these criteria: It must be **delicious, family-friendly, healthy,** and **easy to make.**

1. The recipe is then tested several more times to fine-tune the flavor and ease of preparation, always by the same team member, using the same equipment.

2. Next, another team member follows the recipe as written, **varying the brands of ingredients** and **kinds of equipment.** Even the types of stoves we use are changed.

3. A third team member repeats the whole process **using yet another set of equipment** and **alternative ingredients.**

**By the time the recipes appear on these pages, they are guaranteed to work in any kitchen, including yours. WE PROMISE.**